820.8
B75

T. F. Hoppin del.

I. Fairchild sc.

LANDING OF ROGER WILLIAMS.

THE

RHODE-ISLAND BOOK:

SELECTIONS IN PROSE AND VERSE,

FROM THE WRITINGS OF

Rhode-Island Citizens.

BY ANNE C. LYNCH.

PROVIDENCE:
H. FULLER, 40 WESTMINSTER-STREET.
BOSTON: WEEKS, JORDAN & CO.
1841.

KNOWLES & VOSE, PRINTERS.

TABLE OF CONTENTS.

INDEX OF AUTHORS.

PREFACE.

Mr. Hunter has well remarked, in his eloquent Oration, that "the feeling which in the individual is selfish vanity, diffused and generalised by a community, becomes patriotism," and that "the people of Rhode-Island have a peculiar right to indulge in a State pride." This right will be admitted when it is remembered that in the history of the race, Rhode-Island presents the first instance of a State founded on the broad principles of spiritual freedom, without which, political freedom is but a mockery. Athens was a Democracy when Socrates drank the hemlock, and Rome had scarcely relinquished her title of The Republic, when in one of her provinces, the populace shouted "*Crucify him! crucify him!*"

Neither Greece, Rome, nor the nations of modern Europe had grasped the sublime idea of intellectual liberty, and the glory of founding the first State on this principle remained for an obscure exile on the shores of Narraganset Bay. An eloquent historian has said, "If Copernicus is held in perpetual reverence because, on his death-bed, he published to the world that the sun is the centre of our system, if the genius of Newton has been almost adored for dissecting a ray of light and weighing heavenly bodies as in a balance, let there be for the name of Roger Williams at least, some humble place among those who have advanced moral science, and made themselves benefactors of mankind."

But if we reverence the names of those who have read for us the mysteries of the visible heavens, shall we not reverence more, him who would unbind the fetters that for centuries have cramped the human mind, and shackled the conscience, that connecting link between God and man, and open for us the avenues to the very Heaven of heavens? We say, then, let there be for the name of Roger Williams an *exalted* place,—an illuminated page in the history of Humanity.

Rhode-Island has proved herself worthy of her illustrious founder. In the revolutionary struggle, she was first in the field—and renounced her allegiance to Great-Britain two months before the Declaration of Independence by Congress. The idea of a navy was first suggested in her General Assembly; she furnished two of of the four ships that composed the first American fleet,—many of the officers, and the first and only Admiral. And we need not say how the gallant Perry and his brave Newport followers, sustained on Lake Erie, the honor of that which their fathers had so well begun.

It was thought that the floating *literature* of Rhode-Island contained much that was worthy of preservation; and to give to such passages a "local habitation," has been the object of this publication. From circumstances that could not be controlled, many distinguished names have been omitted; and it is believed that another year, a similar and equally interesting collection might be prepared. TO THE CITIZENS OF RHODE-ISLAND THIS VOLUME IS RESPECTFULLY DEDICATED, BY THE

EDITOR.

Providence, Dec. 1, 1840.

THE RHODE-ISLAND BOOK.

INTRODUCTION TO WHATCHEER.

A POEM.

BY THE HON. JOB DURFEE.

(Addressed to the Rev. Romeo Elton.)

WHAT time, dear ELTON, we were wont to rove,
From classic Brown along fair Seekonk's vale,
And in the murmurs of his storied cove,
Hear barbarous voices still our Founder hail;
E'en then my bosom with young rapture strove
To give to deathless verse the exile's tale,
And every ripple's moan, or breeze's sigh,
Brought back whole centuries as it murmured by.

But soon the brittle dream of youth was gone,
And different labors to our lots were given:
You, at the shrine of peace and glory shone;
Sublime your toils, for still your theme was heaven—

I, upon life's tempestuous billows thrown—
  A little bark before the tempest driven—
Strove for a time the surging tide to breast,
And up its rolling mountains sought for rest.

Wearied, at length, with the unceasing strife,
  I gave my pinnace to the harbor's lee,
And left that Ocean, still with tempests rife,
  To mad ambition's heartless rivalry;
No longer venturing for exalted life,
  (For storms and quicksands have no charms for me,)
I, in the listless labors of the swain,
Provoke no turmoil, and awake no pain.

To drive the team afield, and guide the plough,
  Or lead the herds to graze the dewy mead,
Wakes not the glance of lynx-eyed rival now,
  And makes no heart with disappointment bleed;
Once more I joy to see the rivers flow,
  The lambkins sport, and brindled oxen feed,
And o'er the tranquil soul returns the dream,
Which once she cherished by fair Seekonk's stream.

And when stern winter breathes the chilling storm,
  And night comes down on earth in mantle hoar,
I guide the herds and flocks to shelter warm,
  And sate their hunger from the gathered store;
Then round the cottage hearth the circle form
  Of childhood lovelier than the vernal flower,

Partake its harmless glee and prattle gay,
And soothe my soul to tune the artless lay.

Thus were the numbers taught at first to flow,
  Scarce conscious that they bore a tale along—
Beneath my hand still would the pages grow—
  They were not labor but the joy of song—
Still every line would unsung beauties shew
  In Williams' soul, and still the stream prolong;
Till all enraptured with the theme sublime,
My thoughts spontaneous sought the embodying rhyme.

* * * * * * * * *

WHATCHEER.

CANTO SIXTH.

The winds of March o'er Narraganset's bay
  Move in their strength—the waves with foam are white,
O'er Seekonk's tide the waving branches play,
  The woods roar o'er resounding plain and height;
'Twixt sailing clouds, the sun's inconstant ray
  But glances on the scene—then fades from sight;
The frequent showers dash from the passing clouds;
The hills are peeping through their wintry shrouds.

Dissolving snows each downward channel fill,
  Each swollen brook a foaming torrent brawls,
Old Seekonk murmurs, and from every hill,
  Answers aloud the coming waterfalls;

Deep-voiced Pawtucket thunders louder still;
To dark Mooshausick joyously he calls,
Who breaks his bondage, and, through forests brown,
Murmurs the hoarse response, and rolls his tribute down.

But hark! that sound, above the cataracts
And hollow winds in this wild solitude
Seems passing strange. Who, with the laboring axe,
On Seekonk's eastern marge, invades the wood;
Stroke follows stroke—some sturdy hind attacks
Yon ancient groves which from their birth have stood
Unmoved by steel—and startled at the sound,
The wild deer snuffs the gales—then with a bound

Vaults o'er the thickets, and, down yonder glen,
His antlers vanish—on yon shaggy height
Sits the lone wolf, half peering from his den,
And howls regardless of the morning light—
Unwonted sounds and a strange denizen
Vex his repose—then, cowering with affright
He shrinks away—for with a crackling sound,
Yon lofty hemlock bows, and thunders to the ground.

* * * * * * * * *

LETTER FROM ROGER WILLIAMS,

TO THE GENERAL ASSEMBLY OF RHODE-ISLAND, IN RELATION TO THE SERVICES OF DR. JOHN CLARKE.

[The following characteristic specimen of the composition of Roger Williams, is now for the first time published. This fact it is presumed will give it an interest in addition to its historical value. The Editor is however aware, that at least a brief explanation of the circumstances under which it was written, may be required by those readers who are not familiar with the early history of Rhode Island.

The first charter of the Colony, (the Earl of Warwick's Patent,) was granted in 1643. In 1651, William Coddington went to England, and obtained from the Council of State, a Commission, by which he was made Governor of the Island of Rhode-Island, Canonicut, &c. for life. With this the people were much dissatisfied, and Williams and Clarke were immediately sent by the Colony to England, to procure its repeal, which they accomplished in 1652. Williams returned in 1654, and was in the same year elected Governor. Clarke remained in England as the agent of the Colony, until 1663, when he obtained the Charter of Charles the Second.

It appears from the letters of Williams, that during at least a part of the time while thus absent from home, he was obliged to provide for his own support. He says, in a letter to the town of Providence, written in 1664, "I was unfortunately fetched and drawn from my employment, and sent to so vast a distance from my family, to do your work of a high and costly nature, for so many days and weeks and months together; and there left to starve or steal, or beg, or borrow. But blessed be God, who gave me favor to borrow one while, and to work another, and thereby to pay your debts there, and to come over with your credit and honor, as an agent from you, who had in your name grappled with the agents and friends of all your enemies round about you." It further appears, that he had recourse to teaching as a means of support; and in connexion with this fact, a passage in one of his letters to John Winthrop, written soon after his return, is peculiarly interesting, on account of the proof which it furnishes of his personal acquaintance with his great contemporary, Milton. He says: "It pleased the Lord to call me for some time, and with some persons, to practise the Hebrew, the Greek, Latin, French, and Dutch. *The Secretary of the Council, (Mr. Milton) for my Dutch I read him, read me many more languages.*"

Clarke was absent, in the service of the Colony, twelve years. In 1664, his accounts were audited by the General Assembly, and the sum of £343, 15s. 6d. was found due him, which the Assembly often urged the towns to pay; but that act of justice was not performed during the life of Clarke. His circumstances however were not necessitous,—for he was enabled to die as he lived,—doing good, leaving a Will by which his Estate was to be applied to "the relief of the poor, and bringing up children unto learning."

Clarke was highly respected and esteemed by Williams. Of this fact, an interesting memorial is preserved in the library of Brown University, in a copy of "The Bloody Tenet yet more Bloody," on one of the blank leaves of which, is an inscription in the hand-writing of Williams, in the following words: "For his honored and beloved Mr. John Clarke, an eminent witness of Christ Jesus, against the Bloody Doctrine of Persecution, &c."]

Beloved Friends and Countrymen,

My due respects presented, with hearty desires of your present and eternal prosperity, when this short life is over. I was resolved to have visited you myself, this winter and to have persuaded with arguments of truth and love, the finishing the payments, relating to his Majesty's royal grant and charter to us; but it pleased God, to visit me with old pains and lamenesses, so that sometimes I have not been able to rise, nor go, nor stand. I pray your courteous leave, therefore, of saluting you with these few lines, and your favorable attention to them. On two hinges my discourse shall turn. First, The fairness and equity of the matter. Second, The damage and hazard, if not performed.

As to the first, the fairness of the matter, please you to hear two or three witnesses. The first is Common Honesty and Common Justice in common dealings between man and man. This gives to every man, his due, a pennyworth for a penny, and will cry shame upon us, that Mr. Clarke should be undone, yea, destroyed and ruined, as to this world, for his so great and so long pains, faithfulness and diligence, for which he ought in common justice, to be faithfully satisfied and honorably rewarded, although, it should have pleased God, to have granted him no success, no charter, no favor in the eyes of our sovereign Lord, the King. These very barbarians when they send forth a public messenger, they furnish him out, they defray all payments, they gratify him with rewards, and if he prove lame and sick and not able to return, they visit him and bring him home upon their shoulders, and that many scores of miles, with all care and tenderness.

At the first, Rhode Island, but afterwards the whole Colony requested, employed and sent to Mr. Clarke a commission and credentials sealed, which the King was satisfied, and owned him for our public agent. Now let me say these two things which mine eyes have seen. First when I left Mr. Clarke in England to negotiate the affairs of the whole Colony, I saw with what a low sail he stood along; with what content, patience and self-denial, which course I know he hath continued, having received but little supply from us, nor of his own estate, which he continually wrote for. 2. At our General Assembly when Mr. Clarke's accounts were fairly brought in, and what he had received and what he had borrowed, upon the mortgage of his house and land, to go through our work, the Assembly appointed a committee of able and judicious men to examine the accounts: upon whose report and upon their own further examination and consideration they saw cause to agree upon a very moderate and equal sum to be raised throughout the colony to be discharged unto him.

Worthy Friends, it is easy to find cloaks and

colors for denials or delays to any business we have no minds to. I have visited my neighbors at Providence, this winter. Some say they are sorry and ashamed of the delays and promise to finish it with speed ; some few say, they have done it ; some say they like not some words in the charter ; some say they will pay, if all do ; some are against all government and charters and corporations ; some are not so, and yet cry out against thieves and robbers who take any thing from them against their wills ; some say they will see what became of their former payment, before they will part with any more ; some will see the charter, first, because they hear that Col. Cartwright carried the charter into England with him ; some say, let those that sent Mr. Clarke into England at first, pay him, and some say other things ; but none say aught, in my judgment which answers the witness of Common Honesty : for the whole sum and scope of his Majesty's royal grant and charter to us, is to bestow upon us two inestimable jewels. The first is peace, commonly called among all men, the King's Peace, among ourselves and among all the King's subjects and friends, in this country and wheresoever : and, further, at our agent's most reasonable petition, the King prohibits all his subjects to act any hostility toward our Natives inhabiting with us without our consent, which hath hitherto been otherwise practiced to our continual and great grievance and disturbance.

The second jewel is Liberty. The first, of our spirits, which neither Old nor New England knows the like, nor no part of the world a greater.

2d. Liberty of our persons ; no life, no limb taken from us, no corporeal punishment, no restraint but by known laws and agreements of our own making.

3. Liberty of our Estates, horses, cattle, lands, goods, not a penny to be taken by any rate from us, without every man's free debate by his deputies, chosen by himself, and sent to the General Assembly.

4. Liberty of society or corporation, of sending or being sent to the General Assembly, of choosing and being chosen to all offices and of making or repealing all laws and constitutions among us.

5. A liberty, which other charters have not, to wit, of attending to the laws of England, with a favorable mitigation, viz, not absolutely, but respecting our wilderness estate and condition.

I confess it were to be wished, that these dainties might have fallen from God, and the King, like showers and dews and manna from heaven, gratis and free, like a joyful harvest or vintage, without any pains of our husbandry ; but since the most holy God, the first Cause, hath ordained second causes and means and agents and instruments, it is no more honest for us to withdraw in this case, than for men to come to an Ordinary and to call for the best wine and liquor, the best meats roast and baked, the best attendance, &c. and to be able to pay for all and yet most unworthily steal away and not discharge the reckoning.

My second witness is Common Gratitude, famous among all mankind, yea, among brute beasts, even the wildest and fiercest, for kindness received. It is true, Mr. Clarke might have a just respect to his own and the peace and liberty of his friends of his own persuasion. But I believe the weight that turned the scale with him was the truth of God, viz. a just liberty to all men's spirits in spiritual matters, together with the peace and prosperity of the whole colony. This, I know, put him upon incredible pains and travail, straits and anguish, day and night, himself and his friends and ours, which I believe a great sum of money would not hire him to wade through the like again. I will not trouble you with the allowances, payments, and gratuities of other colonies in like cases. Only let me present you with a famous story out of our English records. Henry the Third, as I remember fell out with the city of London, took away their charter and set a governor over them, which brought many evils and sorrows on them. But Doctor Redman, so called, pacified the King's anger and procured a restitution of their charter, though with great charges and payments of moneys. Now while this Redman lived, they honored him as a father and heaped all possible gratuities upon him ; and when he died they decreed that the Lord Mayor and Aldermen and chief citizens, should, yearly and solemnly visit his tomb, which mine eyes have seen performed in the public walks in Paul's, and I presume, it is practised to this day. I will not trouble you with the application of this story, but present you with my third Witness of the fairness of this matter, which is Christianity, which we all pretend to, though in various and different persuasions. This witness soars high above Common justice and Common gratitude, yea, above all religions. This not only speaks home for due payment and due thankfulness, but of doing good for evil, of paying blessing for cursing, of praying for enemies and persecutors, of selling houses and lands, yea, of laying down lives for others. Common justice would not, Common gratitude would not, least of all will Christianity, employ a public messenger unto a mighty King and there leave him to shift for his living and means to go through so high a service, nor leave him to shift for moneys and to mortgage his house and lands to carry on our business and thus to forfeit and lose them; and lost they are, as all must see, except a speedy redemption save them. Shall we say we are christians, yea but ingenuous or just men, to ride securely, in a troublous sea and time, by a new cable and anchor of Mr. Clarke's procuring and to be so far from satisfying his engagement about them, that we turn him adrift to languish and sink, with his back broke, for putting under his shoulder, to ease us. "Which of you," said Christ Jesus to his enemies "will see an ox or a sheep fall into a pit and not pull it out on the Sabbath day." What beast can labor harder, in ploughing, drawing or carrying, than Mr. Clarke hath done so long a time, and with so little provender? Shall we now when he looks for rest at night, tumble him, by our neglects into a ditch of sadness, grief, poverty and ruin?

Give me leave, therefore to mention my second part or hinge, which is the hazard we run by not a free discharging. For first, one of these three points we must steer on: either Mr. Clarke must patiently lie in the pit and languish and perish, (I speak as to us, for I know there is a paymaster in the heavens who will not fail him ;) or second, some volunteers must patiently put under their shoulders and bear the common burden, which for myself I am ready to do, although I part with my clothes from my back ; or third, the rate must be taken by distraint, in the King's name and authority, and this we know, will be more grievous and chargeable, yet cannot be avoided, if we resolve not to turn rebels or loose vagrants to be catched up by other colonies and governments ; or else to leave our cattle, children, wives and lives to be torn out of our bosoms by the strongest arm, catch who catch can. It is true that honesty and innocency, reason and scripture are infinitely excellent in their way, but are they sufficient to charm, except God please to give his spirit, adders, serpents, foxes, wolves, yea, or to order tame beasts without bit or bridle, as David speaks, by which we all know what David means.

Secondly. If we wholly neglect this business, what will become of our credit ? Rhode-Island, in the Greek language, is an Isle of Roses, and so the King's Majesty was pleased to resent it ; and his honorable commissioners in their last letter to the Massachusetts from the eastward, gave Rhode-Island and this whole colony an honorable testimony which is like to be pointed to the view of the whole world. Shall we now turn our roses into hemlock and our fragrant ointment into carrion? Our own names, in a righteous way ought to be more precious to us, than thousands of gold or silver, how much, infinitely more precious, the name of the most Holy and most High and his holy truth of soul-liberty amongst us.

Thirdly. Again, who knows, what storms and tempests yet abide us. Who now will ever be employed by such masters, in whatsoever straits we may come into? Hath not God taught beasts and birds to be shy of being deceived, especially the second time? How justly shy are the Christians of the Turks, because they are not to be true to Christian dogs, as like dogs they speak. How shy are the Protestants of the Papists, because of their principle and practice, to keep no faith with Heretics. Who will not heareafter be fearful to trust us, when like false Merchants, our bills shall be protested, that all men may take heed how they deal with us.

Fourthly. What a worm and sting of bitterness will it be to us to remember, like Jerusalem in the days of affliction, all our things, such peace, such security, such liberties, for soul and body as were never enjoyed by any Englishman, nor any in the whole world, that I have heard of. If now, for our unthankfulness, it should please God to turn the wind and bring the wheel over us and to clap on our necks those iron yokes which so many thousands and millions of men's necks are under in all nations of mankind, will it not then be as gall to our minds, to call to mind how free we were, yea, to our children's minds, to remember how free their fathers were and might have bequeathed and transferred unto them such precious and invaluable treasures ?

Fifthly. With what indignation, must we needs imagine, will the King himself entertain the thought of such a people, that shall so undervalue and slight the rich and extraordinary favor which it pleased God to put into his royal heart to bestow upon the colony. How hath God been pleased to turn the King's heart toward us, as rivers of water. How hath his favor to us, fallen like dew upon Gideon's fleece, while all the world lies round about us dry and barren of such liberties. What can we now expect but the roaring of a lion, unto such an unrighteous and ungrateful generation ?

Sixthly. And yet if we imagine our mountain to be immoveable by any winds or shakings under heaven, yet we must look higher, to the most High King and Judge of the whole world, in whose most powerful hand we profess to have breath and being, our ways and motions. He hath whips and scourges for colonies and countries, nations and kingdoms, as we have felt in New England this last year, and have dolefully heard, from Old. How have the arrows of the pestilence pierced the hearts of thousands and tens of thousands of our fellow English. How dreadfully hath he mixed the blood of English, Dutch and French with the briny ocean. His jealousy was pleased to cause a black cloud to hover over this country, this last summer. It pleased him to cause this cloud to break and fall on some of our countrymen to the Southard and Westward of us, and then to run to the Northward and Eastward of us to Newfoundland, but not to come near our habitations.

Shall now New England say, shall this colony say, it is for our righteousness—there are no sins that cry in this colony and country for justice to revenge abused mercy?

Worthy friends, the changes of the heavens and the earth have been great and sudden, seen and felt by us all, this winter. Let us not soothe and sing ourselves asleep, with murdering lullabies. Let us provide for changes and by timely humiliation, prevent them. For myself, seeing what I see over all New England, I cannot but say with David, Psalm 119. My flesh trembleth for fear of thee and I am afraid of thy judgments.

I remain, longing after your present and eternal Peace,

ROGER WILLIAMS.

Providence Jan. 1665–6 so called.

CONCERNING SLEEPE AND LODGING OF THE INDIANS.

(From a Key into the Language of America, &c.)

BY ROGER WILLIAMS.

THE GENERALL OBSERVATION.

Sweet rest is not confind to soft Beds, for not only God gives his beloved sleep on hard lodging; but also Nature and Custome gives sound sleep to these Americans on the Earth, on a Boord or Mat. Yet how is Europe bound to God for better lodging, &c.

More particular;

God gives them sleep on Ground, on Straw,
on Sedgie Mats or Boord:
When English Softest Beds of Downe,
sometimes no sleep affoord.

I have knowne them leave their House and Mat,
to lodge a Friend or stranger,

When Jewes and Christians oft have sent
Christ Jesus to the Manger.

'Fore day they invocate their Gods,
though Many False and New:
O how should that God worshipt be,
who is but One and True!

* * * * *

How sweetly doe all the severall sorts of Heaven's Birds, in all Coasts of the World, preach unto men the prayse of their Maker's Wisdome, Power, and Goodnesse, who feedes them and their young ones Summer and Winter with their severall sorts of foode: although they neither sow nor reape, nor gather into Barnes!

If Birds that neither sow nor reape
Nor store up any food,
Constantly find to them and theirs
A maker kind and good!
If man provide eke for his Birds,
In Yard, in Coops, in Cage,
And each Bird spends in songs and Tunes,
His little time and Age!
What care will Man, what care will God
For his wife and children take?
Millions of Birds and Worlds will God
Sooner than his, forsake.

1643.

ROGER WILLIAMS.

BY FRANCES H. WHIPPLE.

Illustrious pioneer of liberty ;
Parent and founder of the truly free !
No treachery deforms thy peerless story ;
No deed of vengeance sullies thy pure glory.
Thy precept and example, hand in hand,
Went like fair sisters o'er the smiling land ;
While the rude Indian, true to Nature's law,
Knew what was good, and trusted what he saw.
He met thee as a brother—gave his land—
And thou gav'st him an open honest hand ;
Nor was his simple nature e'er deceived ;
Nor his proud, noble spirit once aggrieved ;
He was thy brother—thou, 'neath closest scan,
Mid all temptations, wert—an honest man :
Rhode Islanders, with virtuous pride, can tell
Thy line of life has but one parallel—
Thou, and the Son of Peace—the western sage—
Were the twin stars of your illiberal age.
When warlike fame as morning mist shall fly,
And blood-stained glory, as a meteor, die ;
When all the dross is known, and cast away,
And the pure gold, alone, allowed to stay,
Two names will stand, the pride of virtuous men,
Our Roger Williams, and good William Penn.

TO THE WEATHERCOCK ON OUR STEEPLE.

BY ALBERT G. GREENE.

THE dawn has broke, the morn is up,
Another day begun;
And there thy poised and gilded spear
Is flashing in the sun,
Upon that steep and lofty tower
Where thou thy watch hast kept,
A true and faithful sentinel,
While all around thee slept.

For years, upon thee, there, has poured
The summer's noon-day heat,
And through the long, dark, starless night,
The winter storms have beat;
But yet thy duty has been done,
By day and night the same,
Still thou hast met and faced the storm,
Whichever way it came.

No chilling blast in wrath has swept
Along the distant heaven,
But thou hast watched its onward course
And instant warning given;
And when mid-summer's sultry beams
Oppress all living things,
Thou dost foretell each breeze that comes
With health upon its wings.

How oft I've seen, at early dawn,
Or twilight's quiet hour,
The swallows, in their joyous glee
Come darting round thy tower,
As if, with thee, to hail the sun
And catch his earliest light,
And offer ye the morn's salute,
Or bid ye both,—good night.

And when, around thee or above,
No breath of air has stirred,
Thou seem'st to watch the circling flight
Of each free, happy bird,
Till after twittering round thy head
In many a mazy track,
The whole delighted company
Have settled on thy back.

Then, if perchance amidst their mirth.
A gentle breeze has sprung,
And prompt to mark its first approach,
Thy eager form hath swung,
I've thought I almost heard thee say,
As far aloft they flew,—
"Now all away!—here ends our play,
For I have work to do!"

Men slander thee, my honest friend,
And call thee in their pride,

An emblem of their fickleness,
  Thou ever faithful guide.
Each weak, unstable human mind
  A "weathercock" they call;
And thus, unthinkingly, mankind
  Abuse thee, one and all.

They have no right to make thy name
  A by-word for their deeds:—
They change their friends, their principles,
  Their fashions, and their creeds;
Whilst thou hast ne'er, like them, been known
  Thus causelessly to range;
But when thou *changest sides*, canst give
  Good reason for the change.

Thou, like some lofty soul, whose course
  The thoughtless oft condemn,
Art touched by many airs from heaven
  Which never breathe on them,—
And moved by many impulses
  Which they do never know,
Who, 'round their earth-bound circles, plod
  The dusty paths below.

Through one more dark and cheerless night
  Thou well hast kept thy trust,
And now in glory o'er thy head
  The morning light has burst.

And unto Earth's true watcher, thus,
When his dark hours have passed,
Will come "the day-spring from on high,"
To cheer his path at last.

Bright symbol of *fidelity*,
Still may I think of thee :
And may the lesson thou dost teach
Be never lost on me ;—
But still, in sun-shine or in storm,
Whatever task is mine,
May I be faithful to *my* trust
As thou hast been to *thine*.

THE POET.

BY MRS. SOPHIA LITTLE.

He is happy ; not that fame
Giveth him a glorious name ;
For the world's applause is vain,
Lost and won with little pain :
But a sense is in his spirit,
Which no vulgar minds inherit ;
A second sight of soul which sees
Into Nature's mysteries.

Place him by the ocean's side,
When the waters dash with pride ;

With their wild and awful roll
Deep communes his lifted soul.
Now let the sudden tempest come
From its cloudy Eastern home;
Let the thunder's fearful shocks
Break among the dark rough rocks,
And lightning, as the waves aspire,
Crown them with a wreath of fire;
Let the wind with sullen breath
Seem to breathe a dirge of death:
Thou may'st feel thy cheek turn pale;
But he that looks within the veil,
The Bard, high priest at Nature's shrine,
Trembles with a warmth divine.
His heaving breast, his kindling eye,
His brow's expanding majesty,
Show that the spirit of his thought
Hath Nature's inspiration caught.

Now place him in a gentle scene,
'Neath an autumn sky serene;
Let some hamlet skirt his way,
Gleaming in the fading day;
Let him hear the distant low
Of the herds that homeward go;
Let him catch, as o'er it floats,
The music of the robin's notes,
As softly sinks upon its nest

He, of birds the kindliest ;
Let him catch from yonder nook
The murmur of the minstrel brook ;
The stones that fain would check its way
It leapeth o'er with purpose gay,
Or only lingers for a time,
To draw from them a merrier chime ;
E'en as a gay and gentle mind,
Though rough breaks in life it find,
Passeth by as 'twere not so,
Or draws sweet uses out of woe ;
The scene doth on his soul impress
Its glory and its loveliness.

Now place him in some festal hall,
The merry band of minstrels call,
Banish sorrow, pain, and care,
Let graceful sprightly youth be there,
Beauty, with her jewelled zone
And sparkling drapery round her thrown,
Beauty, who surest aims her glance,
When the free motion of the dance
All her varied charms hath stirred,
As the plumage of a bird
Shows brightest when in air he springs,
Spreading forth his sunny wings.
Place the bard in scenes like this,
E'en here he knows no common bliss.

Beauty, mirth, and music twined
Shed bland witchery o'er his mind.
Yet not alone these charm his eyes,
In fancy other sights he spies ;
The ancient feats of chivalry,
Of war's and beauty's rivalry.
That hall becomes an open space,
Where knights contend for ladies' grace.
He sees a creature far more fair
Than any forms around him are ;
One love-glance of her radiant eyes,
The boon for which the valiant dies.
He sees the armored knights advance,
He hears the shiver of the lance,
And then the shot when tourney's done
That greets the conquering champion,
While, kneeling at his lady's feet,
The victor's heart doth scarcely beat,
As, blushing like a new-born rose,
His chosen Queen the prize bestows.

But would you know the season when,
He triumphs most o'er other men,
See him when heart, pulse, and brain,
Are bound in Love's mysterious chain.
Behold him then beside the maid ;
There's not one curl hath thrown its shade
In vain upon that bosom's swell.

All are secrets of the spell
That holds the visionary boy
Breathless in his trance of joy.
And yet no definite desire
Does that strong sob of bliss inspire ;
But sweetly vague and undefined
The feeling that enthralls his mind,
An indistinct deep dream of heaven
Her melting shadowy eye hath given.

These the Poet's pleasures are,
These the dull world cannot share,
These make fame so poor a prize
In his Heaven-enlightened eyes.
What is poetry but this?
A glimpse of our lost state of bliss ;
A noble reaching of the mind
For that for which it was designed,
A sign to lofty spirits given,
To show them they were born for Heaven ;
Light from above, quenched when it falls
Where the gross earth with darkness palls
The fallen soul content to be
Wed to its sad degeneracy ;
But when, like light on crystal streams,
On a pure mind its effluence beams,
How brightly in such spirit lies
An image of the far off skies !

VARIETY OF OPINIONS ON RELIGION.

From the Minute Philosopher.*

BY BISHOP BERKELEY.†

THE variety of opinions about religion is a resting stone to a lazy and superficial mind. But one of more spirit and a juster way of thinking, makes it a step whence he looks about, and proceeds to examine, and compare the differing institutions of religion. He will observe, which of these is the most sublime and rational in its doctrines, most venerable in its mysteries, most useful in its precepts, most decent in its worship? Which createth the noblest hopes, and most worthy views? He will consider their rise and progress, which oweth least to human arts or arms? Which flatters the senses and gross inclinations of men? Which adorns and improves the most excellent part of our nature? Which hath

* Modern Free-thinkers are the very same with those Cicero called *Minute Philosophers*, which name admirably suits them, they being a sect which diminish all the most valuable things, the thoughts, views, and hopes of men: human nature they contract and degrade to the narrow, low standard of animal life and assign us only a small pittance of time, instead of immortality.

[*Minute Philosopher, Dialogue I.*

†Note 1.—See Appendix.

been propagated in the most wonderful manner? Which hath surmounted the greatest difficulties, or shewed the most disinterested zeal and sincerity in its professors? He will inquire, which best accords with nature and history? He will consider, what favors of the world, and what looks like wisdom from above? He will be careful to separate human alloy from that which is divine; and upon the whole, form his judgment like a reasonable free-thinker. But instead of taking such a rational course, one of those hasty sceptics shall conclude without demurring, that there is no wisdom in politics, no honesty in dealings, no knowledge in philosophy, no truth in religion: and all by one and the same sort of inference, from the numerous examples of folly, knavery, ignorance and error, which are to be met with in the world. But, as those, who are unknowing in every thing else, imagine themselves sharp-sighted in religion, this learned sophism is oftenest levelled against christianity. * * * *

Thinking is the great *desideratum* of the present age: and the real cause of whatever is amiss, may justly be reckoned the general neglect of education, in those who need it most, the people of fashion. What can be expected when those, who have the most influence, have the least sense, and those who are sure to be followed, set the worst examples? When youth so uneducated, are yet so forward? When modesty is esteemed pusillanimity, and a deference to years, knowledge, religion, laws, want of sense and spirit? Such untimely growth of genius would not have been valued, or encouraged by the wise men of antiquity; whose sentiments on this point are so ill suited to the genius of our times, that it is to be feared, modern ears could not bear them. But, however ridiculous such maxims might seem to our British youth, who are so capable and so forward to try experiments, and mend the constitution of their country; I believe it will be admitted by men of sense, that if the governing part of mankind, would in these days, for experiment's sake, consider themselves in that old *Homerical* light as pastors of the people, whose duty it was to improve their flock, they would soon find, that this is to be done by an education, very different from the modern, and other maxims, than those of the Minute Philosophy. If our youth were really inured to thought and reflexion, and an acquaintance with the excellent writers of antiquity, we should see that licentious humour, vulgarly called *free-thinking*, banished from the presence of gentlemen, together with ignorance and ill taste; which, as they are inseparable from vice, so men follow vice for the sake of pleasure, and fly from virtue, through an abhorrence of pain. Their minds, therefore, betimes should be formed and accustomed to receive pleasure and pain from proper objects, or, which is the same thing, to have their inclinations and aversions rightly placed. This, according to Plato and Aristotle, was the right education. And those, who, in their own minds, their health, or their fortunes, feel the cursed effects of a wrong one, would do well to consider, they cannot better make amends for what was amiss in themselves, than by preventing the same in posterity.

ON THE PROSPECT OF PLANTING ARTS AND LEARNING IN AMERICA.

Written by Bishop Berkeley during his residence in Newport.

THE muse, disgusted at an age and clime,
  Barren of every glorious theme,
In distant lands now waits a better time,
  Producing subjects worthy fame:

In happy climes, where from the genial sun
  And virgin earth fresh scenes ensue,

The force of art by nature seems outdone,
  And fancied beauties by the true :

In happy climes, the seat of innocence,
  Where nature guides and virtue rules,
Where men shall not impose for truth and sense
  The pedantry of courts and schools :

There shall be sung another golden age,
  The rise of empire and of arts,
The good and great inspiring epic rage,
  The wisest heads and noblest hearts.

Not such as Europe breeds in her decay ;
  Such as she bred when fresh and young,
When heavenly flame did animate the clay,
  By future ages shall be sung.

Westward the course of empire takes its way ;
  The *four* first acts already past,
A *fifth* shall close the drama with the day ;
  Time's noblest offspring is the last.

1730.

THE TRAILING ARBUTUS.

BY SARAH H. WHITMAN.

THERE'S a flower that grows by the greenwood tree,
In its desolate beauty more dear to me,
Than all that bask in the noontide beam
Through the long, bright summer by fount and stream.
Like a pure hope nursed beneath sorrow's wing
Its timid buds from the cold moss spring,
Their delicate hues like the pink sea-shell,
Or the shaded blush of the hyacinth's bell,
Their breath more sweet than the faint perfume
That breathes from the bridal orange-bloom.

It is not found by the garden wall,
It wreaths no brow in the festive hall,
But dwells in the depths of the shadowy wood,
And shines like a star in the solitude.
Never did numbers its name prolong,
Ne'er hath it floated on wings of song,
Bard and minstrel have passed it by
And left it in silence and shade to die.
But with joy to its cradle the wild-bees come
And praise its beauty with drony hum,
And children love in the season of spring
To watch for its early blossoming.

In the dewy morn of an April day,
When the traveler lingers along the way,
When the sod is sprinkled with tender green
Where rivulets water the earth unseen,
When the floating fringe on the maple's crest
Rivals the tulip's crimson vest,
And the budding leaves of the birch-tree throw
A trembling shade on the turf below,
When my flower awakes from its dreamy rest
And yields its lips to the sweet south-west,
Then, in those beautiful days of spring,
With hearts as light as the wild-bird's wing,
Flinging their tasks and their toys aside,
Gay little groups through the wood-paths glide,
Peeping and peering among the trees
As they scent its breath on the passing breeze,
Hunting about among lichens grey
And the tangled mosses beside the way,
Till they catch the glance of its quiet eye
Like light that breaks through a cloudy sky.

For me, sweet blossom, thy tendrils cling
Still round my heart as in childhood's spring,
And thy breath, as it floats on the wandering air,
Wakes all the music of memory there.
Thou recallest the time when, a fearless child,
I roved all day through the wood-paths wild,
Seeking thy blossoms by bank and brae
Wherever the snow-drifts had melted away.

Now, as I linger mid crowds alone,
Haunted by echoes of music flown,
When the shadows deepen around my way
And the light of reason but leads astray,
When affections, nurtured with fondest care
By the trusting heart, become traitors there;
When weary of all that the world bestows
I turn to nature for calm repose,
How fain my spirit in some far glen
Would fold her wings mid thy flowers again!

THE LANGUAGE OF A FUTURE STATE.

BY ROWLAND G. HAZARD.

It is probable that in the future and more perfect state of existence, we shall possess a means of social intercourse free from ambiguity—that the pleasure of advancement will be increased by its consequent acceleration—that when deprived of the material organs, words and signs will no longer be employed—in a word, that the language of ideality, which a partial improvement of our faculties has here exhibited, will then be so perfected, that terms will be *entirely* dispensed with, and thought be there communicated without the intervention of any medium to distort its meaning or sully its brightness—that ideas will there flow directly from mind to mind, and the soul be continually exhilarated by breathing a pure congenial atmosphere, inhaling feeling, poetry, and knowledge.

This conjecture derives a further plausibility, from the consideration that our present language seems especially adapted to things material, that in the purely physical sciences we can communicate ideas with great accuracy and precision—that the difficulty of doing this increases in proportion as our feelings and the qualities of mind enter into the subject to which we endeavor to apply it, and when they become exclusively its objects, it almost entirely fails. Poetry has accomplished much more than the other forms in portraying the passions, sentiments, and all the more striking and complicated mental phenomena, but even that has shed but a feeble light over a small portion of this interesting field of research, or in bright but fitful gleams, shown the undefined vastness not yet explored. Our present language, then, is wholly inadequate to a subject, which of all others must most interest a world of spirits, as if it were intended only to carry us to the point from which we are there to start—to give us a glimpse of the infinite regions, which imagination has not yet traversed—the exhaustless sources of thought which mind still possesses, while the language of ideality has here accomplished just enough in the exhibition of the subjects of our internal consciousnesss, to assure us that it also possesses the elements of a power, which when matured, may become the fitting instrument to gather the treasures of that unexplored immensity. But may we not go farther, and say that we have even here a foretaste, or at least a nearer approach to this angelic pleasure? Have we not witnessed the soul in all its purity and vigor, throwing off the trammels which words impose on its highest action, and, as if anticipating its conscious destiny, in a transport of impassioned thought and feeling, almost entirely discarding the usual mode of expressing them, when the eloquence of the eye anticipates the tongue, when every feature kindles with emotion, and the whole countenance is as a transparency lighted with its glowing conceptions? It is then that terms are most nearly dispensed with, and it is in this sympathetic mingling of thought and sentiment that we enjoy the purest poetry which warms the soul in its earthly tabernacle. Those who have known the raptures of such converse and have felt its exalting influence, will regard it as worthy a place in a higher sphere, and be willing to admit it to their most entrancing reveries of elysian bliss. Does not this view lend a delightful confirmation to our hypothesis? But the argument derives yet additional strength from the consideration that this faculty, this power of silent, yet vivid expression, seems somewhat proportioned to moral excellence, or increases as the spiritual predominates over the material part of our natures—that in most men it is at best but dimly visible—that in those of the finer grade of intellect, whose feelings have been cultivated, whose purity has never been sullied by corroding care and ignoble pursuits, nor their sensibility blunted by too rude collision with the world, it becomes more apparent; while in the sex of finer mould, who are elevated above these degrading influences—whose feelings are more pure—whose sentiments are more refined—and whose spirits are more etherial, it manifests itself with a softened splendor, to which that of angels, may well be supposed, only another step in the scale of a magnificent progression. It is to the superiority which woman has in this expressive language; to her command of this direct avenue to the finer feelings, that we must attribute her influence in refining and softening the asperities of our nature. And it is owing to the possession of this element of moral elevation, that while the finest and strongest reasoning of philosophy has, in this respect, acccomplished so little, that woman has accomplished so much. She possesses not the strength which has been exhibited by some masculine minds, nor perhaps even the brilliancy which has emanated from others; but the influence which they respectively exert on society appears in strange disproportion to the *apparent* causes. The one is as the sun, which sheds his strong beams upon the waters, and the waves proudly reflect his dazzling brilliancy; the other, as the moon, whose milder light melts into the ocean; glows through all its depths; heaves its mighty bosom, and elevates it above its common level.

The refined subtleties of an Aristotle, or the glowing sublimities of a Plato, though presented to us with all the fascinations of a high-toned morality, and clothed in the imposing grandeur of a lofty and commanding eloquence, are dim and powerless to that effusion of soul, that seraphic fervor, which with a glance unlocks the avenues to our tenderness, which chides our errors with a tear, or winning us to virtue with the omnipotence of a charm, irradiates its path with the beaming eye, and cheers it with the approving smile of loveliness. And hence, too, it is, that the degree in which this influence is felt, and its source appreciated, is justly considered as the test of civilization and refinement.

Is there not in this mild, gentle, silent, persuasive, yet dissolving and resistless influence, a charm which bears witness to its celestial character? Do we not recognize in it a similarity to that of heaven, and if we have ascribed it to its proper cause, does not this similarity at once stamp our speculation, if not with the seal of a moral certainty, at least with the impress of a cheering probability?

THE LIVING-DEAD.

BY WILLIAM J. HOPPIN.

"Yet one doubt
Pursues me still, lest *all* I cannot die:
Lest that pure breath of life, the spirit of man
Which God inspired, cannot together perish
With this corporeal clod: then in the grave,
Or in some other dismal place, who knows,
But I shall die a living death?"
[PARADISE LOST, B. X.

I DREAMED that Death had froze
This young and glowing frame:
But He, whose grasp the pulse could chill,
Had failed the hidden sense to still,
Or loose the prisoned flame:
Had fled away
From his half-slain prey
And left the conscious Soul bound to the mouldering clay.

I heard a requiem sung—
A prayer to Heaven said—
A sigh breathed forth—perchance a tear
Moistened the pall above my bier—
But soon they left the dead:
  And soon forgot,
  For there came not
One friendly footstep back to cheer the lonely spot.

The years, which once seemed fleet,
How slowly they passed by!
The winter's storm did hoarsely rave
Long, long, ere round my gloomy grave
The summer breeze did sigh:
  But the doleful knell
  Would often tell
That another shade had fled in death's dark land to dwell.

Oh, thrice, thrice happy soul!
Like mine it was not doomed
To pass ten thousand years away—
Undying Spirit chained to clay,
Immortal Thought entombed!
  Can Hell bestow
  A fiercer woe
Than this, through countless years to die and still to know?

* * * * * *

Now centuries had past ;
The funeral knell was o'er,
The sons forgot where their fathers lay
For I heard the plough-share grate its way
Where the grave-stone stood before ;
   And the reapers tread
   Above my head,
And sing their merry songs among the silent dead.

And there a forest sprang
From the ground where we reclined.
The lofty boughs spread high in Heaven—
For I heard them groan by the tempest driven,—
The roots our dust entwined :
   But a fire at last
   O'er the forest passed
And each firm root decayed beneath the withering blast.

And there, deep, still, alone,
In a barren waste I lay,
Hushed was the song of the cheerful bird,
And nought of human sound I heard,
All, all, had passed away—
   And the years stole by
   So silently,
I thought that Nature slept in mortal lethargy.

* * * * * *

Hark ! thunder wakes the world,
It rives the trembling sod !
The burning Universe doth tell
This is the voice of the Archangel,
This is the Trump of God !
Aye, He hath spoke—
The trance is broke—
" Ye Living-Dead arise !" Shuddering with fear, I woke.

THE ANNIVERSARY OF AMERICAN INDEPENDENCE.

BY THE HON. JONATHAN RUSSELL.

It is a magnificent spectacle to behold a great people annually crowding their temples to consecrate the anniversary of their sovereignty. On this occasion the heart of every true American beats high with a just and noble pride. He still hears the illustrious Fathers of his Country, appealing to the Supreme Judge of the World for the rectitude of their conduct, declare that the United States "are, and of right ought to be, Free and Independent." The black catalogue of injury, abuse, contempt, and crime, which exhausted forbearance and drove us to resistance, rushes on his mind. He passes in review those great men who then burst upon the world, and who, endowed with every virtue and every talent which could fit them for the arduous task in which they engaged, appeared to be expressly commissioned by Heaven to rule the storm of revolution. It was then, indeed, that human nature, which for eighteen centuries had appeared nearly to have lost those qualities which alone ennoble it, emerged at once from its degradation, and recovered the lustre with which it shone in the happiest days of antiquity.

On the islands of the Adriatic, the mountains of Biscay, and the rocks of Uri, the spirit of Liberty had indeed successively sought a refuge ; but driven at last from all that could delight her on earth, she had already flapped her wings on the glaciers of Switzerland, and was taking her flight towards Heaven. The American people rose—they burst their fetters—they hurled them at their oppressors—they shouted they were FREE. The sound broke across the Atlantic—it shook the fog-wrapt island of Britain, and re-echoed along the Alps. The ascending spirit heard it—she recognized in it the voice of her elect, and holding her course westward, she rejoicing saw her incense rise from a thousand altars. Her presence assured our triumph. Painful, however, was the struggle, and terrible the conflict which obtained that triumph—our harbors filled with hostile fleets—our fields ravaged—our cities wrapt in flames—a numerous veteran and unprincipled enemy let loose upon us—our army thinned by battles, wasted by sickness, disgusted by treachery and desertion—a prey to every species of privation, and reduced to the last misery next despair. Even then, however, this little army shewed themselves worthy the holy cause for which they contended. Driven from Long-Island—from the heights of Harlem—from White Plains—pursued from post to post even to beyond the Delaware—they would often turn upon their insulting foe—and mingling their blood with the melting lava of the cannon's mouth, foretel them of *Trenton*, *Germantown*, and *Monmouth*.

But it was not in the ardent conflicts of the field only, that our countrymen fell; it was not the ordinary chances of war alone, which they had to encounter. Happy, indeed, thrice happy, were WARREN, MONTGOMERY and MERCER; happy those other gallant spirits who fell with glory in the heat of battle, distinguished by their country, and covered with her applause. Every soul, sensible to honor, envies rather than compassionates their fate. It was in the dungeons of our inhuman invaders; it was in their loathsome and pestiferous prison-ships, that the wretchedness of our countrymen still makes the heart bleed. It was there, that hunger, and thirst, and disease, and all the contumely which cold-hearted cruelty could bestow, sharpened every pang of death. Misery there wrung every fibre that could feel, before she gave the blow of grace which sent the sufferers to eternity. It is said that poison was employed. No, there was no such mercy there—there nothing was employed which could blunt the susceptibility to anguish, or which by hastening death could rob its agonies of a single pang. On board one of these prison-ships above *eleven thousand* of our brave countrymen are said to have perished. She was called the *Jersey*. Her wreck still remains, and at low ebb presents to the world its accursed and blighted fragments. Twice in twenty-four hours the winds of Heaven sigh through it, and repeat the groans of our expiring countrymen; and twice the ocean hides in her bosom those deadly and polluted ruins, which all her waters cannot purify. Every rain that descends washes from the unconsecrated bank the bones of those intrepid sufferers. They lie naked on the shore accusing the neglect of their countrymen. How long shall gratitude and even piety deny them burial? They ought to be collected in one vast ossory, which shall stand a monument to future ages of the two extremes of the human character; of that depravity, which, trampling on the rights of misfortune, perpetrated cold and calculating murder on a wretched and defenceless prisoner; and that virtue which animated this prisoner to die a willing martyr for his country. Or rather, were it possible, there ought to be raised a *Colossal Column*, whose base sinking to *Hell*, should let the murderers read their *infamy* inscribed on it; and whose capital of *Corinthian* laurel ascending to *Heaven*, should show the sainted ***Patriots*** that they have triumphed.

Deep and dreadful as the coloring of this picture may appear, it is but a faint and imperfect sketch of the original. You must remember a thousand unutterable calamities, a thousand instances of domestic as well as national anxiety and distress, which mock description. You ought to remember them; you ought to hand them down in tradition to posterity, that they may know the awful price their fathers paid for freedom. * * * * *

1800.

OUR COUNTRY.

BY WILLIAM J. PABODIE.

OUR Country!—'tis a glorious land—
With broad arms stretched from shore to shore;—
The proud Pacific chafes her strand,
She hears the dark Atlantic roar;

And nurtured on her ample breast,
  How many a goodly prospect lies;
In Nature's wildest grandeur drest,
  Enamelled with her loveliest dyes.

Rich prairies, decked with flowers of gold,
  Like sun-lit oceans roll afar;
Broad lakes her azure heavens behold,
  Reflecting clear each trembling star;
And mighty rivers, mountain-born,
  Go sweeping onward, dark and deep,
Through forests, where the bounding fawn
  Beneath their sheltering branches leap.

And cradled 'mid her clustering hills,
  Sweet vales in dream-like beauty hide,
Where Love the air with music fills,
  And calm Content and Peace abide;
For Plenty here her fullness pours,
  In rich profusion o'er the land;
And sent to seize her generous stores,
  There prowls no Tyrant's hireling band.

Great God! we thank Thee for this home—
  This bounteous birth-land of the Free;
Where wanderers from afar may come,
  And breathe the air of Liberty;—

Still may her flowers untrampled spring,
Her harvests wave, her cities rise ;
And yet till Time shall fold his wing,
Remain earth's loveliest Paradise !

GERMAN LITERATURE.

BY SARAH H. WHITMAN.

It has been said that "it is in the German nature duly to honor every thing produced by other nations." Our countrymen, we fear, are in danger of becoming, like the English, too exclusively national. We could wish that they had a little more of the German cosmopolitanism. Perhaps it is natural that whenever any attempt is made by a portion of the community to lead the public mind to new trains of thought or modes of action, to introduce new theories or point out new fields for exertion or enterprise, that an antagonist party should spring up, whose tendency it is to resist all innovation. Perhaps it is a wise provision of nature that has thus furnished every age with its sentinels and warders, as well as with its bold and adventurous pioneers ; and provided they conduct themselves fairly and discreetly in their vocation, we have no desire to see their office annulled, or to interrupt them in its rightful exercise. Let the sentinels give challenge to all new claimants, but let them not refuse admittance to any who can furnish a fair passport, or make out a clear title to be received within their guarded citadel.

Since the efforts which have recently been making to introduce the German literature among us, it is not unusual to hear the most unqualified, indiscriminate opposition expressed to the study of a language of unequalled copiousness, flexibility and force, rich in every department of its literature, and entitled, in the opinion of the first European scholars, to an equal estimation with our own noble mother tongue. Yet we are rejoiced to discover, even in the bitterness of its opponents, an indication of the increasing interest with which it is regarded among us; we are in no way disturbed by the fear that its subtleties, refinements and abstractions, should exert an evil influence on our national character, the individuality of which seems in no danger of being neutralized by such antagonist principles, though it may perchance be favorably modified by them. The Germans, it is true, have their faults; but these faults, it has been well said, are as good as virtues to us, since being the exact opposites of our own, they may teach us most important lessons.

The opposers of German literature are fond of preferring the claims of common sense to those of philosophy; of elevating the actual over the ideal. They descant much and rather vaguely against Transcendentalism. They tell us of the folly of believing in innate ideas, and triumphantly quote Locke and his "tabula rasa." They are afraid of all vagueness and my sticism, and tremble like children at the shadowy appearances seen in the twilight. They will have nothing to do with that which they cannot handle. They have faith in nothing which they cannot fully comprehend. They like to see all objects clearly and sharply defined in the broad day-light of the understanding. Yet in the shadowy, twilight regions of the imagination, we may behold much that is then only visible. The near glare of the sun conceals from us those far lights of heaven, that are forever burning in the vaults of space; even as the acute shrill sounds of day prevent us from hearing the deep voices of nature. The Shekinah, which was by day only a cloud of smoke, became by night a pillar of fire.

In literature, their favorite models are those writers who are most remarkable for clearness, polish, and precision. They seem to prefer vigorous, rather than comprehensive thinkers;—writers whose vision is clear but limited; who deal manfully with facts and events, but care not to penetrate beyond the surface of being, showing us things as they are, without questioning of the how and why. They love to pace steadily and safely along with the "smooth tongued Addison, the stately Johnson, and the sublime Burke," never deviating from the beaten path, and looking upon all who go down in diving-bells, or mount in balloons, as hair-brained tempters of fate.

They fear all new aspects of truth, and gravely tell us, that "it is better with our fallible natures and limited capacities, to rest upon certain ideas and opinions that have been received as plausible, rejecting all speculations upon subjects which can never be decided, nor farther developed, while the soul remains in the thralls of flesh."

Supposing a reflective mind could bring itself to act upon this suggestion, or rather to cease from acting, for ourselves we know of no opinions that have been universally received as "plausible," and did we know any such, we could not receive them as truths, until they had been submitted to the test of our own reason. Who shall tell us that any man or class of men have monopolized the right of thought? What is truth to another is not truth to us until our own understanding has verified it. Whatever danger there may be in leaving every man to decide for himself, there is surely far less than in any attempt to restrict the individual right of opinion, through regard to expediency or respect for authority.

We could not, if we would, have every man a philosopher, and we think there need be little fear, that our countrymen will become infected with any undue fondness for abstract researches. The mind that has never tried to grasp the great problems of human life and destiny, that has never sought to wrest a reluctant meaning from the hieroglyphic characters inscribed on the broad page of nature, needs no such restriction; the mind that has done this, will hardly be checked in its onward impulse by the "*cui bono*" of the utilitarian. It sounds almost like mockery to ask one who has ever caught a single ray of the warm, living light of the sun of truth, to satisfy himself with the frippery, gilt-paper toy of "plausibility." These timid counsellors remind us of Solomon's slothful man, who keeps housed and says, "there is a lion in the street, if I go forth I shall be slain." There are some who cannot be thus easily restrained; they must "go forth," even at the worst of perils—they must meet the lion, and wrestle with it as they may—and often do they find, that when they look their formidable foe calmly in the face, he loses all his terrors, and becomes at once harmless and tractable.

These persons are constantly opposing revelation to nature, and faith to reason. We cannot agree with them in apprehending any danger to Christianity from the investigation of calm, tolerant, philosophic spirits, who fear not to look at both sides of a question, lest they should meet with something opposed to established and time-hallowed opinions. The timid faith that fears to question, cannot satisfy us,—such assent is far worse than honest denial. The only *fatal* skepticism, as it seems to us, is that of the man who wants faith in the human soul, and fears to trust its promptings.

For ourselves, we rejoice in the increasing number of those who are willing to follow truth wherever she may lead them, in the spirit of that child-like confidence and perfect love which casteth out fear. We look for the time when philosophy shall aid in reconciling reason and faith, not by depressing faith, but by elevating reason. When we shall be able to interpret, in all its beautiful simplicity, the word of Him who taught us to read the gospel of Nature, to observe the lilies of the field, and to seek for the kingdom of heaven within our own hearts.

The enforcement of this self-reliance, this faith in the power of the individual to discover for himself truth, is one of the leading heresies of which the "New School" is accused. Yet the highest stars of heaven may be seen mirrored within the single drop of dew that trembles within the heart of a violet.

This faith in truth and nature, this desire to free the mind from its slavery to creeds and conventionalities, though the growth of no particular school, has, it is true, within the last twenty years, been more profoundly felt and more earnestly inculcated, than at any former period. It gives a tone to all the noblest literature of the day, and is slowly but surely working a change in the character of the times. It is this which prompted the obnoxious declaration of Dr. Channing that "Man is great as man, be he what and where he may." This is what was implied by Emerson, when he said, "let a man plant himself on his instincts, and the whole world will come round to him," or in other words, work in harmony with him. It is this which illumines every page of Carlisle, as with the glory of an inspired scroll, and imparts to the apocalyptic reveries of Swedenborg whatever they possess of vivifying and converting energy.

This doctrine, which was taught by a few sincere and simple spirits, amid the darkest gloom of Jewish superstition and bigotry, has caused one of the most true hearted believers of our own day to assert that the vital truths of Christianty are too deeply inwrought into the very nature of the human soul to be in any danger from a free and zealous examination into the true character of the Christian miracles. It is this growing conviction which is beginning to render all persecution for opinions sake as disgraceful as it ever was futile, and this it is, above all, which is teachiug the instructors and guardians of youth, that the great objects of education are not to be achieved by the exhibition of facts or the inculcation of theories, but by developing and strengthening the powers of the soul for individual and independent action.

Much, though not all of this, is we think attributable more or less directly to the Germans. Much that in our own literature is but faintly and dimly shadowed forth, is in this developing itself in free and luxuriant growth. In the German literature, to use one of their own expressive phrases, " man finds himself." The " sweet sad music of humanity" pervades every department of it. In its deep earnest philosophic spirit ; in its fearless, trusting, transparent simplicity ; in the holy fervor of its poets ; the serene, spiritual, far-reaching gaze of its theologians and moralists, we may find much which even the rich, classical literature of England cannot supply.

To us, Germany has ever been a bright land of promise since first in early youth we listened with kindling heart and eager sympathy to the tidings which Mde. De Stael had brought us of a people, who in an age of artificiality, had dared to follow the suggestions of their own spirits and to show us nature as she had mirrored herself within their own hearts. And now, having possessed ourselves of the golden Key which is to unlock for us this rich world of thought, we cannot but glory in our new-found treasure, and endeavour to win others to become partakers of our joy.

SUGGESTED BY ALLSTON'S PICTURE OF JEREMIAH AND BARUCH IN THE PRISON.

BY SARAH S. JACOBS.

A prisoner prince ! Each haughty limb
Bespeaks thy high descent ;
Nor can a dungeon's gloom bedim
One noble lineament.

To fetter thee, did they not dare?
Thou can'st not be contented there
A captive with that kingly air,
Stern and magnificent.
Thou listenest a lute to hear,
Struck by some minstrel's skill;
Thou dreamest,—that strain so soft and clear
Makes thee a monarch still.
The dungeon is forgotton now,
A smile illumines lip and brow,
Again thy subjects round thee bow,
Obedient to thy will.

Methought there breathed upon my ear
In low, deep strain,
A greater than a King is here,
Look thou again!

A prisoner *poet*—thou the free,
The impatient of control,—
Of more than regal majesty,
The majesty of soul;—
And must *thou* pining linger here
Till grief her last indignant tear
Has shed: while o'er thee, year by year,
A captive's sorrows roll?
What by thy listening ear is heard?
What stirs thy poet heart?
Hath water's voice or note of bird
In that deep dream a part?

Or musest thou some noble song,
The story of thy bitter wrong,
In hurrying tide to pour along,
The triumph of thine art?

Then a whisper came—*he dreameth not now*
Of wood or wave;
Nor his, the patriot's burning vow,
His land to save.

A prisoner *prophet*—thus at last
Thy mission grand, I know;
Thine is no shadow of the past,
Nor grasp of present woe,
Thou man of destiny sublime
Over whose mind's gigantic prime
The surging waves of coming time
Successive ebb and flow;
The summer sea is not more bright,
The summer cloud more free
Than thou, all radiant with the light
Of conscious Deity.
Around thee might the thunders peal,
Beneath, the solid prison reel,
Unbroken still thy spirit's seal,
Unmoved thy gaze would be.

* * * * * *

It makes the gentle tears to fall,
The tears that fall to bless,

Thy thoughtful face, oh, scribe, with all
Its loving winningness.
Passionless intellect alone
Around the Prophet's form is thrown,
And might untold ;—but all thine own
Fair youth, the happiness
To sit and listen and record
Unnoticed by his side,
And treasure every wondrous word,
With reverence dignified ;
Gazing, meanwhile with earnest grace
Like some babe angel in the face
Of seraph in the Holy place,
With love and lowly pride.

MORAL SUBLIMITY ILLUSTRATED.

BY THE REV. FRANCIS WAYLAND, D. D.

Philosophers have speculated much concerning a progress of sensation, which has commonly been denominated the emotion of sublimity. Aware that, like any other simple feeling, it must be incapable of definition, they have seldom attempted to define it ; but content with remarking the occasions on which it is excited, have told us that it arises, in general, from the contemplation of whatever is vast in nature, splendid in intellect, or lofty in morals. Or, to express the same idea somewhat varied, in the language of a critic of antiquity, "that alone is truly sublime, of which the conception is vast, the effect irresistible, and the remembrance scarcely if ever to be erased." But although philosophers only, have written about this emotion, they are far from being the only men who have felt it. The untutored peasant, when he has seen the autumnal tempest collecting between the hills, and, as it advanced, enveloping in misty obscurity, village and hamlet, forest and meadow, has tasted the sublime in all its reality; and, whilst the thunder has rolled and lightning flashed around him, has exulted in the view of nature moving forth in her majesty. The untaught sailor boy, listlessly hearkening to the idle ripple of the midnight wave, when on a sudden he has thought upon the unfathomable abyss beneath him, and the wide waste of waters around him, and the infinite expanse above him, has enjoyed to the full, the emotion of sublimity, whilst his inmost soul has trembled at the vastness of its own conceptions. But why need I multiply illustrations from nature? Who does not recollect the emotions he has felt, whilst surveying aught in the material world, of terror or of vastness?

And this sensation is not produced by grandeur in material objects alone. It is also excited on most of those occasions in which we see man tasking, to the uttermost, the energies of his intellectual or moral nature. Through the long lapse of centuries, who, without emotion, has read of LEONIDAS and his three hundred throwing themselves as a barrier before the myriads of Xerxes, and contending unto death for the liberties of Greece!

But we need not turn to classic story to find all that is great in human action; we find it in our own times and in the history of our own country. Who is there of us that even in the nursery has not felt his spirit stir within him, when with child-like wonder he has listened to the story of WASHINGTON? And although the terms of the narrative were scarcely intelligible, yet the young soul kindled at the thought of one man's working out the deliverance of a nation. And as our understanding, strengthened by age, was at last able to grasp the detail of this transaction, we saw that our infantine conceptions had fallen far short of its grandeur. O! if an American citizen ever exults in the contemplation of all that is sublime in human enterprise, it is when, in bringing to mind the men who first conceived the idea of this nation's independence, he beholds them estimating the power of her oppressor, the resources of her citizens, deciding in their collected might that this nation should be free, and through the long years of trial that ensued, never blenching from their purpose, but freely redeeming the pledge which they had given, to consecrate to it, "their lives, their fortunes and their sacred honor."

It is not in the field of patriotism only that deeds have been achieved to which history has awarded the palm of moral sublimity. There have lived men, in whom the name of patriot has been merged in that of philanthropist; who, looking with an eye of compassion over the face of the earth, have felt for the miseries of our race, and have put forth their calm might to wipe off one blot from the marred and stained escutcheon of human nature; to strike off one form of suffering from the catalogue of human woe. Such a man was HOWARD. Surveying our world, like a spirit of the blessed, he beheld the misery of the captive, he heard the groaning of the prisoner. His determination was fixed. He resolved, single handed, to guage and to measure one form of unpitied, unheeded wretchedness, and, bringing it out to the sunshine of public observation, to work its utter extermination. And he well knew what this undertaking would cost him. He knew what he had to hazard from the infections of dungeons, to endure from the fatigues of inhospitable travel, and to brook from the insolence of legalized oppression. He knew that he was devoting himself upon the altar of philanthropy, and he willingly devoted himself. He had marked out his destiny, and he hastened its accomplishment, with an intensity "which the nature of the human mind forbade to be more, and the character of the individual forbade to be less." Thus he commenced a new era in the history of benevolence. And hence the name of HOWARD will be associated with all that is sublime in mercy, until the final consummation of all things.

Such a man is CLARKSON, who looking abroad, beheld the sufferings of Africa, and, looking at home, saw his country stained with her blood. We have seen him, laying aside the vestments of the priesthood, consecrate himself to the holy purpose of rescuing a continent from rapine and murder, and erasing this one sin from the book of his nation's iniquities. We have seen him and his fellow philantropists for twenty years never waver from their purpose. We have seen them persevere amidst neglect, and obloquy, and contempt, and persecution, until the cry of the oppressed, having roused the sensibilities of the nation, the "Island Empress" rose in her might and said to this foul traffic in human flesh, thus far shalt thou come, and no farther.

THE BARON'S LAST BANQUET.

BY ALBERT G. GREENE.

O'ER a low couch the setting sun had thrown its latest ray,
Where in his last strong agony a dying warrior lay,
The stern old Baron Rudiger, whose frame had ne'er been bent
By wasting pain, till time and toil its iron strength had spent.

"They come around me here, and say my days of life are o'er,
That I shall mount my noble steed and lead my band no more;
They come, and to my beard they dare to tell me now, that I,
Their own liege lord and master born,—that I, ha! ha! must die.

And what is death? I've dared him oft before the Paynim spear,—
Think ye he's entered at my gate, has come to seek me here?
I've met him, faced him, scorned him, when the fight was raging hot,—
I'll try his might—I'll brave his power; defy, and fear him not.

Ho! sound the tocsin from my tower,—and fire the culverin,—
Bid each retainer arm with speed,—call every vassal in,
Up with my banner on the wall,—the banquet board prepare,—
Throw wide the portal of my hall, and bring my armor there!"

An hundred hands were busy then,—the banquet forth was spread,—
And rung the heavy oaken floor with many a martial tread,
While from the rich, dark tracery along the vaulted wall,
Lights gleamed on harness, plume and spear, o'er the proud old Gothic hall.

Fast hurrying through the outer gate the mailed retainers poured,
On through the portal's frowning arch, and thronged around the board.
While at its head, within his dark, carved oaken chair of state,
Armed cap-a-pie, stern Rudiger, with girded falchion, sate.

"Fill every beaker up, my men, pour forth the cheering wine,
There's life and strength in every drop,—thanksgiving to the vine!
Are ye all there, my vassals true?—mine eyes are waxing dim;—

Fill round, my tried and fearless ones, each goblet to the
brim.

Ye're there, but yet I see ye not. Draw forth each trusty
sword,—
And let me hear your faithful steel clash, once around my
board:
I hear it faintly:—Louder yet!—What clogs my heavy
breath?
Up all,—and shout for Rudiger, 'Defiance unto Death!'"

Bowl rang to bowl,—steel clanged to steel,—and rose a
deafening cry
That made the torches flare around, and shook the flags on
high:—
"Ho! cravens, do ye fear him?—Slaves, traitors! have
ye flown?
Ho! cowards, have ye left me to meet him here alone!

But *I* defy him:—let him come!" Down rang the massy
cup,
While from its sheath the ready blade came flashing half-
way up;
And with the black and heavy plumes scarce trembling on
his head,
There in his dark, carved, oaken chair, Old Rudiger sat,
dead.

A VISIT TO NIAGARA.

BY THE REV. FREDERICK A. FARLEY.

ONE of the most delightful journeys which our country offers, is that which takes the traveller through some of the most fertile and beautiful regions of the state of New York, from its great Commercial Capital to the falls of Niagara. The picturesque and romantic shores of the Hudson—the wonderful region of Saratoga, where the entire soil seems to be underlaid with fountains of healing water of almost every variety—the rich valley of the Mohawk, presenting to the eye at every turn a view of exhaustless fertility and exquisite beauty—the remarkable gorge at Little Falls, where the various elements of mountain and river scenery, the deep ravine, the towering precipice, the craggy, overhanging cliffs, the huge masses of rock scattered and flung here and there as if in very sport by the rushing torrents which once broke through this narrow pass, and having worn their way along found an outlet below—Trenton, that spot of unrivalled beauty—the vast lakes which seem to open upon your astonished gaze, so far inland are you, like the great ocean itself—and finally that

Great Cataract, which the world over is its chief wonder—all these, to say nothing of what human enterprise and skill have accomplished through this entire region, in rail-roads and canals, towns and villages, agriculture and manufactures, conspire to excite a deep enthusiasm in the mind of the beholder, to quicken and to exalt it.

In the sublime description of the creation, in the book of Genesis, we read that "The Spirit of God moved upon the face of the waters." But may not the same language be applied to the whole of external nature? Does not the soul amid its various scenes, whether on land or sea, by day or night, as it looks above, around, or beneath, feel that the Spirit of God is there?

In the sweet flow of the gentlest stream, winding way between the high banks, covered with verdure, and flowering shrubs and vines trailing their branches in the water—or the rush of the nobler river along its deeper channel cut among lofty highlands, whose bases rest undisturbed amid its depths, and whose dark shadows project themselves over its surface;—or the lofty mountain, bathing its altar peak in the clouds;—within the black and tangled forest, whose rich foliaged arches and columns make it a fit cathedral for sublimest worship; or on the outspread, ever-rolling ocean, whether in the calm or in the storm,—always mighty, always vast, ever symbolizing the eternal; in these, and in every varied scene of nature, may the mind of man recognise the all present Spirit of God. And to every mind thus attuned to this the loftiest inspiration which the contemplation of nature can awaken, ever fresh and delightful will be its varying visions, as they by turns come.

But beyond and above all other objects in nature which I have ever yet gazed upon, none has ever filled me with such an overpowering sense of the presence of God, as that of the Great Cataract of the west. I may not essay a description of that which the finest geniuses which have ever visited those stupendous Falls have shrunk from attempting, from a mere consciousness of inability to do any adequate justice to the subject—but simple gratitude to God, that I have been permitted to see this wondrous work of His hands, bids me attempt to express some of the emotions with which the sight filled me, and which, whenever felt, must make a visit to Niagara one of the holiest pilgrimages of life.

I reached the Falls from below. That is, I coasted up the broad expanse of Lake Ontario, one of those great inland seas, in themselves among the wonders of our western hemisphere, and sailed up the river to Lewiston. Thence a short rail-road of fifteen miles takes you to the Falls. As the road lies in a great degree near the river, and sometimes upon the very brink of the beetling precipices which overhang it, the traveller is gradually prepared to behold in a right frame of mind the great object of his journey. The water is seen to be of a most peculiar and vivid green, of a hue which of itself forms one of the unsettled problems of the region—streaked here and there with foam, and broken into eddies and whirlpools ; while the banks gradually become more and more lofty, jagged and wild. The spray of the cataract, which we had observed, while on the lake before we entered the river, rising like a vast column of cloud in the early morning air, was now seen as the day advanced broken into ever-shifting and fantastic wreaths of mist, or light feathery clouds floating in and scattered by the sun. So perfectly in keeping seemed all the scenery as we approached the Falls, to what I had imagined of the Falls themselves, that notwithstanding the curiosity which every step of our progress made only the more intense, not one feeling of disappointment for a moment cast its shadow over my soul, when at length I stood, a silent, rapt beholder of this "wonder of the waters," as its name of Indian origin expressively denotes.

"The roar of waters!—from the headlong height
Niagara cleaves the wave-worn precipice;
The fall of waters! rapid as the light
The flashing mass foams shaking the abyss;
"The hell of waters! where they howl and hiss,
And boil in endless torture; while the sweat
Of their great agony, wrung out from this
Their Phlegethon curls round the rocks of jet
That gird the gulf around, in pitiless horror set,

And mounts in spray the skies, and then again
Returns in an unceasing shower, which round,
With its unemptied cloud of gentle rain,
Is an eternal April to the ground,
Making it all one Emerald:—how profound
The gulf! and how the giant element
From rock to rock leaps with delirious bound,
Crushing the cliffs!"——*

The river in its descent from Lake Erie has become a noble stream of deep and crystal water of a mile in breadth, flowing on calmly towards the north—until, when nearly a mile above the Falls, it

* Childe Harold, Canto IV. I have taken the liberty to substitute "Niagara" in the second line for "Velino."

begins to encounter vast ledges of submerged rocks, by which it is gradually disturbed, and soon exchanges its soft and silvery smoothness for a rushing, roaring waste of waters. In its whole course thence to the Falls, it presents the appearance of the ocean lashed by a tremendous tempest—the foaming waves leap to an amazing height—mighty whirlpools are formed—deep and shifting eddies—jets d'eaux of every graceful figure rise from the edges of rocks which lift their heads near or above the surface—and thus, broken and chafed, it rushes on with prodigious force and rapidity, and finally hurls its monstrous volume of waters into the abyss.

In the midst of the wildest uproar of these wondrous rapids, there are the sweetest and most romantic islets interposing their quiet and lovely verdure and foliage, in striking contrast with the confusion and din around them. While Iris* Island, covering an extent of more than forty acres, crowned with the primæval forest, flanks and overhangs the vast boiling gulf, and breaks the river in twain ;—thus forming on one side the Great American Fall, and on the other the Crescent, or Horse-Shoe Fall. A bridge of ingenious construction, passing directly

* Or, Goat Island.

over these rushing rapids to the length of six hundred and fifty feet, enables you to visit this island of most picturesque and surpassing beauty, and enjoy the various and sublime views which it offers of the rapids and the Cataract.

I walked first to the American Fall, and looked from the piazza of a small building upon this scene of wonders. After a few minutes enjoyment of the magnificent coup d' œil here presented, I went to the very brink of the Fall, and soon discovered just over the edge of the precipice a small projecting slab which might serve for a single foothold ;—stepping upon this, and grasping firmly with my right hand a naked stump, among the shrubbery which grows upon the margin, I swung myself over, and gazed down, down, into the very gulf into which that vast mass of waters was rushing. When I returned to a firmer position upon the solid earth, I had no words for my emotions, and a tribute of tears alone gave them vent.

The river, at the usual place of crossing just below the American Fall, is contracted between stupendous natural walls to the width of half a mile ; and as you are swept downward in your frail boat by the deep and strong current, you forget all danger amid the astonishing scenery which surrounds you. On your left and rear is the American Fall, nine hundred feet in breadth, and leaping one hundred and sixty feet perpendicularly into the abyss—its whole surface dyed and striped in ribands of every prismatic hue, throughout its entire descent. Above and before you, is the Grand Crescent, twenty-one hundred feet in breadth and about one hundred and seventy-five high—whose mighty fall lashes the pool beneath into a rich creamy foam, boiling like a gigantic cauldron—from which rises the spray in unceasing clouds, and upon which rainbows are painted in their most delicate and deepest tints ;—while midway across the cataract, the water seems in its descent to encounter here and there projecting ledges of rock, which throw out the spray at right angles, like volumes of smoke from the mouths of some ordnance hidden beneath. You are now beneath the most stupendous Cataract of the world ; and by the testimony of accomplished travellers who have climbed the Alps, the Himalaya, and the Pyramids, and visited every shore and every sea, before you is the chief wonder of, the most magnificent sight on earth.

And I can truly say, that whencesover or at whatever hour, I viewed them, "the Spirit of God" seemed to me moving "upon the face of those waters"—the one thought ever present to, ever forced upon my mind, at every turn, at every point of view, was—GOD! Never did I feel so strikingly the littleness of man—never so thrillingly the presence of the Supreme! Nor was it always in one attribute, or one class of attributes, and that of the more awful kind. For never was there a place where the beautiful and the sublime, the soothing and the terrible, were so blended. You cross upon a frail and trembling bridge an arm of the rapids, till you completely overlook from the projecting termination of that daring structure the raging and foaming cauldron beneath—and you turn to the island which you have just left, and see all the witching romance of most sequestered streets, and the most perfect rural beauty. You prostrate yourself upon the brink of Table Rock, that you may send your gaze far under that beetling canopy of stone into the dim caverns behind and below—and the rainbow, spanning the abyss in remarkable entireness and beauty meets your delighted eye, and tells of hope and peace amid that wild tumult and terror. You descend to the edge of the gulf below—you creep along the slippery and insecure footpath which leads far above it—you look upward, and the overhanging rock which shoots its tablet of stone far outward beyond you, seems just ready to fall—you press on, till amid a blinding whirlwind and torrents of spray you pass "within the veil," behind the Great Sheet of water where a single mis-step, or a moment's loss of self-command would hurl you into that roaring abyss,—but soon you emerge in safety, and discover skirting this very scene of terror the most striking displays of natural beauty—the sparkling of transparent waters in the sun—their pure and brilliant emerald as it passes the brink of the crescent glittering like an ever-forming and majestic gem, in beautiful contrast with the snowy whiteness of the foam around it—while in all directions the prismatic tints are shining clearly out. Thus God in His Power—and God in His Benignity and Love, meet you at every turn!

Nor is it by sight alone, that Niagara speaks to the soul of its all-present God. I have been at midnight, with no other light but that of the pale stars, and stood on the very verge of that mighty cataract.—All was indistinct to the eye,—save as its spectral foam was reflected in the dim starlight;—but to the ear, and through that to the soul, how thrilling, how solemn and grand were its voices!

Miss Sedgwick, in one of her beautiful tales makes one of its youthful characters—as he stands upon

Table Rock, where all had been hushed into silence by the magnificent vision before them—exclaim—"What is it, Mother, that makes us all so silent?" The reply is in part in the sublime words of the sacred historian—"It is in the spirit of God moving upon the face of the waters!" It is in this new revelation to our senses of his power and majesty which ushers us, as it were, into His visible presence, and exalts our affections above language." Well, indeed, might man be hushed before that glorious manifestation of the presence of his maker,—and when he has mused in silence, until he has caught the full import of the wondrous scene, he will prostrate his spirit in adoration and worship.

Stupendous, however, as is Niagara—ever-flowing, unwearied, unexhausted in its career, as seems that wondrous cataract—symbol, as I have called it, of the Eternal—how clear is it, that there is another thought upon the subject quite as striking and true. Stupendous as it is, it will have an end. Ever-flowing as is that rushing torrent, it will yet be hushed and gone. Symbol of eternity as it now appears, the symbol will fade before the reality. Nay, while I write, I feel that to us it may be a symbol of something of the deepest, personal interest;—of Time, ever-flowing;—and we, we, are upon its current!

To some of us, it may be, so calmly and gently are we gliding on, that its soft and mirror-like surface scarce seems to be floating us away; but the rapids are before us, and each one in turn must pass, as do the successive drops which compose that mighty volume of waters, into the dark, deep gulf! How delighting, how cheering to the soul, that over that dark, deep gulf, has the Sun of Righteousness lighted up the rainbow of Hope!

FROM THE MARTYRDOM OF ST. PETER AND ST PAUL.

BY THE REV. GEORGE BURGESS.

* * * * * *

Behold the forum's throng, the murm'ring street,
The bath, the bridge, the scenes where millions meet.
Each land has exiles there, for none is free;
All loathe the lords, as all have bowed the knee.
Numidia's swarthy son, subdued at length;
The blue-eyed German with his giant strength;
The graceful chiefs of some devoted host
That bled to guard their Britain's lovely coast;
The crouching form where lurks a bitter heart
That yet may teach how true the Parthian dart;
The Hebrew doomed a tenfold scorn to brook,

A tenfold anguish writhing in his look ;
All, all are here : nor theirs the pride to share,
Waked by this pomp of famed, and grand, and fair :
Their's but to plod the way of wily gain,
Or curse the arts that forged and decked the chain.
And wish one equal day one equal field,
Where nought should win, but lance, and sword and shield.

In joy returned from wars of distant lands,
Marked by his scars, the legion's veteran stands ;
The tall pretorian nods his helm of pride,
The massy pavement ringing to his stride ;
Solemn and slow, the stately priests ascend,
In worship not their own to strike or bend ;
The patient sculptor wakes to gradual view
Ideal forms and dreams not all untrue ;
The expecting crowd surround the patron's gate ;
The morning chariot rolls in gilded state ;
The light buffoon with idle jibe and jest,
Scans the nerved athlet's mighty arm and chest ;
Morn warms with life the city's utmost vein,
And every passion holds its wonted reign.

* * * * * *

O'er the vast throng a brief, deep silence sank ;
From the fallen prey astonished vengeance shrank ;
Then, hoarse and faint, arose the heartless call,
" So let the foes of Rome and Cæsar fall !"
Alone stood Simon :——— * *
Round his torn limbs the sevenfold bands they wound,

And his swollen forehead almost pressed the ground ;
They strained each cord, they cleft each gushing vein,
They plied each weapon of distracting pain :
Each pang's, each torture's work, amazed they viewed,
Each pang, each torture pierced, but none subdued.
But ere the hammer heaved its closing blow,
Chill, chill and faltering rolled the life blood slow ;
Ere half their bootless rage the torments spent,
On angel wings the sweet release was sent.

* * * * * *

And thou, who comest from thine own Northern land
On Roman dust in memory's trance to stand,
When thine enchanted feet have learned to stray
Through all this classic waste of old decay ;
Imperial halls half hid mid lowly vines,
Fair imaged saints that smile o'er conquered shrines ;
Arch far o'er arch, where moss and ivy grow,
Columns that stood while empires fell below,
The walks where fables morning shadows spread,
The graves and trophies of the mighty dead :
When thou hast wandered arts impassioned slave,
And owned what might to man the maker gave ;
When o'er thy soul the spirit of the past
All its thick cloud of solemn dreams hath cast,
Then seek with me, some spot where fancy's ear
The apostle martyr's echoing voice may hear ;
And from that spot behold, behind, before,
As round a rock, the sea of ages roar.

Thou hast a bark to cross the stormy tide ;
Thou too must follow, and perchance may'st guide :
From first to last one sovereign power extends,
And all the light the worth the glory blends ;
It filled those breasts, it centered in that hour,
It crowned that spot : knowest thou that sovereign power ?
Hast thou not felt, oh ! feel its presence now,
And hast thou felt, in meek devotion bow :
And when thy words, in home's delighted hall,
The tale, the scenes, the dreams of Rome recall,
Then be thou strong to walk where such have led
Arm for the field where worthier bosoms bled ;
And find thy bliss to see amidst thy sphere,
In life, in death, the closing conquest near.

ON THE VALUE OF LIBERAL STUDIES.

BY WILLIAM G. GODDARD,

Professor of Belles Lettres in Brown University.

LIBERAL Studies are adapted not only to moderate an extravagant desire for wealth, but to aid in establishing the true principles upon which wealth should be expended. In a country like our own, these principles, if well understood, are apt to be very imperfectly applied. The primitive stages in the progress of refinement we have long since passed.

Leaving far in the rear the cheap pleasures, the simple habits, and the unpretending hospitalities of our forefathers, we have engaged, it is to be feared, somewhat too largely, in the career of ambitious splendor, and inappropriate magnificence. Impelled too often by the unworthy desire to surpass our neighbors, in some matter of mere external embellishment, we lavish thousands, in multiplying around ourselves the elements of an elegant and selfish voluptuousness. I am distressed by no morbid apprehensions concerning the progress of luxury in our land. I am terrified by no apparition of monopoly. I utter no response to the vulture cry of the Radical, now heard in the distance. I am far from thinking that the opulent ought to diminish their expenses. I believe that, with signal advantage, they might increase them. But in the selection of those objects of embellishment which it is in the power alone of abundant wealth to command, I am not singular in contending that the decisions of a simpler and better taste ought not to be disregarded. Is it not a matter of just reproach, that of all the apartments in our mansion houses, the library is generally the most obscure, and often the most ill furnished ; and that the fashionable upholsterer is allowed to absorb so much of our surplus revenue, that hardly any is left for the Painter and the Statuary ? In all this, there is manifested a melancholy disproportion—an imperfect apprehension of some of the best uses to which wealth can be applied. In the spirit of an austere philosophy, it is not required that we should dispense with those costly ornaments which can boast no higher merit than their beauty ; but it would be hailed as a most benignant reform, if, in the arrangements of our domestic economy, there could be traced a more distinct recognition of the capacities and destinies of man as an intellectual and moral being—as a being endowed with Imagination and Taste—with Reason and with Conscience. How few among us cultivate the Fine Arts ! How few understand the principles upon which they are founded—the sensitive part of our nature to which they are addressed ! To this remark, the imperfect knowledge of Music, which, in obedience to the authority of fashion, is acquired at the boarding school, forms no exception. It may still be affirmed, that we have among us no *class* who delight in Music as one of their selectest pleasures ; who gaze with untiring admiration upon the miraculous triumphs of Painting ; who are filled with tranquil enthusiasm by the passionless and unearthly beauty of Sculpture. And is not this to be lamented? Do we not thus estrange ourselves from sources of deep and quiet happiness, to which we might often resort for solace, and refreshment, and repose? To these sources of happiness there is nothing in the nature of our political institutions, or of our domestic pursuits, which sternly forbids an approach. We have, it is true, no titled aristocracy; and property does not, as in the land of our forefathers, accumulate in large masses, and descend, undivided, through a long line of expectant proprietors. But there is scarcely a city, a town, or a village, in this land, where some could not be found, blessed with every requisite but the disposition, to acquire a genuine relish for the fine arts. Nay, more—in our larger cities, all of which boast their commercial prosperity, and some their Athenian refinement, why should not the masters of the pencil and the chisel be employed to furnish for the private mansion those precious decorations, which alone are secure from the capricious despotism of fashion? By thus expending some portion of their superabundant wealth, the opulent would drink deeply of those finer joys which are perversely left unapproached by the indolent, the voluptuous and the profligate. Thus, too, would they gather around themselves almost inexhaustible means of winning others from sordid pursuits, to the contemplation of the imperishable glories of Genius and of Art.

* * * * *

The value of Liberal Studies, in counteracting the influence of politics upon the individual and social character of our countrymen, deserves next to be considered. Politics is with us becoming a distinct, though not very reputable trade; the strife for power is hardly less eager than the strife for gain; a new code of political ethics has been established, for the accomplishment of pliant consciences; and, almost without an exception, the public men of both parties, and of all parties, tired of waiting for popularity to run after them, are now eager to run after popularity. Who now so intrepid as to dare to take his stand, upon grave and well defined principles? In these days of meek condescension to the will of the people, and of affected reverence for their good sense, how few care to lead public opinion aright! how many pusillanimously follow it, when they know it to be wrong! How few, alas! will forego the vulgar trappings of office for the sustaining consciousness, that by no sacrifice of principle or of dignity, did they ever seek to win them! I would fain believe that the days of the republic are not numbered; but I am not without sad forebodings of her fate, when aspirants for popular favor are such utter strangers to the grace of an erect and manly spirit as to be solicitous rather to appropriate to themselves, at any cost, some transient distinction, than to await, with unfaltering rectitude and unforfeited self-respect, the judgments of coming times; when the man of wealth, and talent, and social consideration, outstrips the Radical, in zeal for pestilent doctrines and mischievous projects; in fine, when it is incorporated in the creed of the politician, that the people are always in the right; in other words, that public opinion is not only the standard of taste, but the keeper of conscience!

* * * * *

Well might I be deemed an unfaithful advocate of Liberal Studies, if, in estimating their value, I yielded no tribute of applause to the solid provision which they make for independent individual happiness; for that happiness which is enjoyed, not so much amid the hum and shock of men, as amid the solitude of Nature and of Thought. Living in a land where "men act in multitudes, think in multitudes, and are free in multitudes," we are constantly tempted to forget the mysterious individuality of our being ; to go out of ourselves for materials of enjoyment ; to fritter away our sensibilities, and to debilitate our understanding, amid the false and hollow gaieties of the crowd. I contend for no severe estrangement from the joys of a chaste and elegant conviviality ; for no exclusive intercourse with forms of inanimate beauty ; for no fearful communion with the mysteries of the inner spirit. But I deprecate habits and tastes which are impatient of seclusion ; which destroy all true and simple relish for nature ; which scorn all quiet pleasures ; which abhor alike the composure and the scrutiny of meditation. As means of reforming tastes and habits thus uncongenial to virtue and to happiness, I can hardly exaggerate the importance of Liberal Studies. I ascribe to them, however, no power to teach rooted sorrow the lesson of submission ; to succor virtue amid mighty temptations ; to dispel the awful sadness of the inevitable hour. These are the victories of Christian Faith ; the grand, and peculiar, and imperishable evidences of its power. But I challenge for Science and for Letters the noble praise of reclaiming us from the dominion of the Senses ; of lightening the burden of Care ; of stimulating within us the undying principles of the Moral Life.

DRESS.

BY MRS. ELEANOR B. BURGES.

Some men pretend that dress is only meant
As a protection from the heat and cold ;
In which some little vanity is blent,
Which shows itself in jewels and in gold,
Well,—let their worships think so—I'm content—
Tho' I another story shall unfold.
If this be all, the Indians in their skin
Of beast, the palm of wit and sense must win.

Their woollen manufacturers are bears,
Their colors lasting, "dyed when in the wool."
Man gives the brute a stab, and then he tears
His coat from off his back with one strong pull ;
Better than broadcloth superfine it wears,
And fits—tho' made without the tailor's rule.
If it be true that dress is but a cover,
This is the shortest method ten times over.

And more becoming too,—for then it shows
That man indeed is "Lord of the Creation,"
And gives him "l'air distingue."—Now his clothes
But mix and mingle every rank and station ;
That may have been the object—for who knows
From cut or color, what's a man's vocation ?
Black once belonged to priests and undertakers,
But now 'tis worn by all men save the Qakers,

Women have long been laughed at—'tis a shame ;
I'm sure there's no occasion for a smile,
If they endure it longer they are tame,
For now they have been silent a great while.
Of wit and moralist it is the aim
Fair woman from this passion to beguile ;
"The vanity of dress" their ceaseless cry,
While woman has dressed on without reply.

But woman has a genius wondrous keen,
She reads in dress what sages read in stars,
She need not go beyond this world I ween,
To learn of Fate or Destiny—which bars
Or seems to bar us in. Much can be seen
In millinery shops, which helps or mars
The "March of Mind"—for upon Fashion's banner,
New truths are written in a certain manner.

Now I have come to my great proposition,
Dress is a hieroglyphic of the mind !
I do maintain against all opposition,
Champollion in Egypt did not find
So deep a mystery—his supposition,
For what I know, is learnedly refined.
But for dark things we need not go to Egypt
And look on marble temples or see crypt.

No!—if you wish a puzzle look on me!
Tell, if you can, why I wear this or that ?
My coat, if I have one, is *thus*, you see,

And my cap *so*, and *so* my shoe and hat ;
" It is the style" you say—why that may be ;
But why such style ? you cannot tell, " that's flat."
Dress is the spirit of the age corporeal !
Sometimes 'tis "l'esprit solide," sometimes "gloriole."

It was the fashion once as you all know,
To wear stick heels and powder and brocade,
Now this was hieroglyphical to show
The mind on stilts and formally arrayed
In others' manufacture—all was so
Stately and stiff; the mind and dress both made
For courts and courtiers only to be used ;
By common people both would be abused.

Then simple thought and dress came in together
In that Emporium of both " Belle France."
The same age saw pomatum, powder, feather,
And the Bastile demolished—at a glance,
Toupees went off with heads. Now whether
They thought them symbols, and that 'twould advance
The cause of Freedom, thus to change the Fashion,
I do not know ; but thus they long did dash on !

When Kings threw off their royal purple dress,
Their majesty went too, with these externals,
And their corporeal part became, I guess,
What the conundrum has it. The diurnals
Soon found, that in those ermine robes, no less

Than in the man, was royalty—the journals
Made war on privilege, and shirts with ruffles,
Which led to riots and to horrid scuffles.

When they dethroned their rulers, then their hair
Was " a la Brutus"—male and female head
Both cropp'd—and Madame Tallien, the fair,
Who lectured to the learned—when she read
She dressed quite masculine, and had the air
Of the *most noble sex*, and all she said
Was just like what she wore—which clearly shows
She thought there was some meaning in her clothes.

And when against the Turks rose up the Greeks,
Why then all heads, we know, were " a la Grec."
And this thing lasted, I believe, for weeks,
And curls were flowing o'er each graceful neck
For Greece and not for beauty! He who seeks
To know the hobby of the day, and spec-
Ulate on what is coming, need but know
The latest Paris mode and what's "the go!"

And thus you see, that Fashion is symbolical.
It is an art, a science, quite profound;
Its characters are always metaphorical,
In which the spirit of the Age is found,
And, if you will not think me tautological,
And in my words see less of sense than sound,
I'll say again, that dress is hieroglyphical,
And hats and caps and SLEEVES are ideographical!

THE EXISTENCE OF GOD.

BY THE REV. JONATHAN MAXCY, D. D.

The nobler part of man clearly evinces this great truth that there must be a God uncaused, independent and complete. When we consider the boundless desires and the inconceivable activity of the soul of man, we can refer his origin to nothing but God. How astonishing are the reasoning faculties of man! How surprising the power of comparing, arranging and connecting his ideas! How wonderful is the power of imagination! On its wings, in a moment, we can transport ourselves to the most distant part of the universe. We can fly back, and live the lives of all antiquity, or surmount the limits of time, and sail along the vast range of eternity. * * *

This great Being is every where present. He exists all around us. Wherever we turn, his image meets our view. We see him in the earth, in the ocean, in the air, in the sun, moon and stars. We feel him in ourselves. He is always working round us; he performs the greatest operations, produces the noblest effects, discovers himself in a thousand different ways, and yet the real God remains unseen. All parts of creation are equally under his inspection. Though he warms the breast of the highest angel in heaven, yet he breathes life into the meanest insect on earth. He lives through all his works, supporting all by the word of his power. He shines in the verdure that clothes the plains, and the lily that delights the vale, and the forest that waves on the mountain. He supports the slender reed that trembles in the breeze, and the sturdy oak that defies the tempest. Far in the wilderness, where human eye never saw, where the savage foot never trod, there he bids the blooming forest smile, and the blushing rose open its leaves to the morning sun. There he causes the feathered inhabitants to chant their wild notes to the listening trees and echoing mountains. There nature lives in all her wanton wildness. From the dark stream that rolls through the forest, the silver-scaled fish leap up, and dumbly utter the praise of God. Though man remains silent, yet God will have praise. * * *

When you survey this globe of earth, with all its appendages; when you behold it inhabited by numberless ranks of creatures, all moving in their proper spheres, all verging to their proper ends, all animated by the same great source of life, all supported at the same great bounteous table; when you behold not only the earth, but the ocean and the air, swarming with living creatures, all happy in their situation; when you behold yonder sun, darting a vast blaze of glory over the heavens, garnishing mighty worlds, and waking ten thousand songs of praise; when you behold unnumbered systems diffused through vast immensity, clothed in splendor, and rolling in majesty; when you behold these things, your affections will rise above all the vanities of time; your full souls will struggle with extacy, and your reason, passions and feelings, all united, will rush up to the skies, with a devout acknowledgment of the existence, power, wisdom and goodness of God. Let us behold him, let us wonder, let us praise and adore. These things will make us happy. They will wean us from vice, and attach us to virtue.

1795.

TO THE AUTUMN FOREST.

BY WILLIAM J. PABODIE.

Resplendent hues are thine!
Triumphant beauty—glorious as brief!
Burdening with holy love the heart's pure shrine,
Till tears afford relief.

What tho' thy depths be hushed!
More eloquent in breathless silence thou,
Than when the music of glad songsters gushed
From every green-robed bough.

Gone from thy walks the flowers!
Thou askest not their forms thy paths to fleck;—
The dazzling radiance of these sunlit bowers
Their hues could not bedeck.

I love thee in the Spring,
Earth-crowning forest! when amid thy shades
The gentle South first waves her odorous wing,
And joy fills all thy glades.

In the hot Summer time,
With deep delight thy sombre aisles I roam,
Or, soothed by some cool brook's melodious chime,
Rest on thy verdant loam.

But O, when Autumn's hand
Hath marked thy beauteous foliage for the grave,
How doth thy splendor, as entranced I stand,
My willing heart enslave!

I linger then with thee,
Like some fond lover o'er his stricken bride;
Whose bright, unearthly beauty tells that she
Here may not long abide.

When MY last hours are come,
Great God! ere yet life's span shall all be filled,
And these warm lips in death be ever dumb,
This beating heart be stilled,—

Bathe thou in hues as blest—
Let gleams of Heaven about my spirit play!
So shall my SOUL to its eternal rest,
In glory pass away!

FROM A DISCOURSE,

DELIVERED ON THE SECOND CENTENNIAL ANNIVERSARY OF

THE SETTLEMENT OF PROVIDENCE.

BY THE HON. JOHN PITMAN.

IT was in the summer of 1636, that Roger Williams, banished from Massachusetts, and warned by the friendly voice of the Governor of Plymouth, sought an asylum beyond the territories of Christian men. Forsaking his plantation at Seekonk, he embarked on the Pawtucket, approaching the western shore, was greeted with the friendly *whatcheer* of the natives, and doubling the southern promontories directed his little bark where a beautiful cove received the waters of the Moshassuck. Here he landed; beneath the forest boughs, and beside a crystal spring, he sought refreshment and repose; here he offered up his thanks to God, that when the hearts of his civilized brethren were alienated, he had found sympathy, protection and sustenance from the rude children of nature; and here in the thankfulness of his heart for past mercies, and full of pious hope for the future, he fixed his abode and named it *Providence.* The spring remains and sends forth its refreshing waters, the only local memorial of the place of his landing and settlement. The principle remains which brought him hither, unimpaired by time, its truth tested and enforced by the experience of two hundred years, and now constituting, not the reproach of a small, despised, and persecuted colony, but the glory and happiness of millions of freemen.

To commemorate this event, to honor this founder, to dwell on some passages of our history which may help us to appreciate the perils, toils, and sufferings of the Narragansett pilgrims, to discharge a portion of that debt which is due to the memory of our worthy ancestors, to cherish those principles which have made us what we are, and which we hope to transmit as their best inheritance to posterity —for these high purposes we are here assembled.

The dimensions of our State are humble; the

politician of the day, in his estimate of relative power, regards us as of small account; but in the history of mind, in the progress of intellectual and moral excellence, what is there, from the dawn of the reformation, unto the present day, of more importance than the principle which gave birth to our State, and has pervaded all our institutions?

We celebrate annually the birth day of our independence, and long may we continue to celebrate it, not because we should delight in the story of wrong and outrage, of battles fought and battles won; but because it tells the price of freedom, and shows how dearly it was purchased. But of what value is independence? Why rejoice that we have broken a foreign yoke, if it should only prepare us for a domestic yoke of greater oppression. Unless our liberty is preserved, the story of the revolution would only cause us to lament that so much blood had been shed, and so much suffering endured in vain. It is liberty which gives to our annual celebrations their greatest charm, their best propriety. It is that true liberty may be well understood, and duly appreciated, that lessons of wisdom may, on this day, be inculcated, that they may be enforced by examples of heroism and patriotism which abounded in those glorious days of our republic—it is for these great ends, that this day should be commemorated, from age to age, by all that can impress the youthful mind, or animate and purify maturer years.

If, then, liberty is the charm which awakens all hearts, shall we forget him who proclaimed, and suffered for proclaiming a principle which is the corner stone of freedom, and who made it the basis of our State ? a principle without which perfect civil liberty cannot long exist, and the existence of which will ultimately destroy tyranny in church and state ?

Civil liberty may exist to a certain extent without religious liberty ; but where religious liberty exists, her triumph insures the triumph of civil liberty. Destroy the hierarchy and you have removed the firmest support of the throne ; if the throne continues, it must be filled, not by an arbitrary monarch, but a constitutional king, who executes the will of the people.

Look at the history of despotism, and you will find a two-fold cord has bound the human race. *Force* has enslaved the body, and *superstition* the mind. What but this has prevented, in our day, the regeneration of Spain and Portugal ? And what but this has deformed the history of South-American liberty and independence ? The mind, free to act upon religious topics, unawed by councils, popes, or

10*

prelates, will not acknowledge the divine, or, in modern phrase, the *legitimate* right of kings. It was for this reason that the reformation accomplished so much for civil liberty, and that the puritans of England were the great reformers in church and state.*

How long would the principles of the reformation have continued if the principle of Roger Williams had not been engrafted upon them? The pope was quite as good a head of the church as Henry the eighth; quite as tolerant as Elizabeth, or James the first. The yoke of the Lords Bishops, of England, was not more intolerable than the dominion of the Lords brethren of Massachusetts.

Take the most liberal sect among us, and give it dominion over all others, make it the religion of the State, give it patronage, and tythes from the property of all, and how long would it be before fit instruments would be found to conspire against our civil liberties, or a people servile enough to wear the chains of imperial and ecclesiastical bondage?

* "So absolute, indeed, was the authority of the crown, that the precious spark of liberty had been kindled, and was preserved by the puritans alone; and it was to this sect, whose principles appear so frivolous, and habits so ridiculous, that the *English owe the whole freedom of their Constitution*."—*Hume's England, chap.* 40, *Elizabeth's reign.*

Many fear that they behold already, among us, the signs of political degeneracy, in the influence of that patronage which extends to every village of the Union; but if you should add to this a permanent power to feed the bodies, and sway the souls of men, how long, think you, we should celebrate, with the spirit of freemen, the anniversary of our independence, or take any pleasure in perpetuating the evidences of our degeneracy?

I say, then, and without fear of contradiction from those who give it due reflection, that the principle of liberty of conscience, which was first promulgated in Massachusetts by Roger Williams, which he boldly maintained before all their magistrates and ministers, and which, driven from thence, he brought to these shores, and made the inheritance of our children—that this principle is of more consequence to human liberty than *Magna Charta*, and constitutes, of itself, a bill of rights which practically secures the enjoyment of all.

What honors, then, should cluster around his name, who, in an age when the most enlightened failed to perceive the simple and majestic proportions of this great truth, perceived it with a clearness, and illustrated it with a force, to which no succeeding age has added, and which now constitutes so much of the freedom and happiness of our common country. If we cannot compare with our sister States in the empire of matter, we may venture to compare with them in the empire of mind, and challenge them to produce a principle, in their settlement or progress, more vital than this to the perpetuation of our liberties. * * * *

TO A SMILING INFANT.

BY SAMUEL W. PECKHAM.

" Pibi semper sine nubibus aether
Integer, et large diffuso lumine ridat."—*Lucretius.*

" A PENNY for your thoughts," fair child!
A penny! aye, I'd part
With countless treasures, could I read
The secrets of that heart ;
Could I but feel the careless joy
That fills thy laughing eyes,
And know the gay imaginings
That o'er thy fancy rise.

I've pondered o'er the classic tomes
Of Roman and of Greek,
Intent through an illusion dark,
Some hidden truth to seek ;

And as its light with thrilling power
   Flashed from the beaming line,
A rapture which the scholar's life
   Alone imparts, was mine.

But oh, 't were bliss beyond compare,
   To read on infant thought
The pure impress of God's own truth,
   Ere sin its blight has wrought ;
To see its power to fill the soul
   With unalloyed delight,
And throw o'er fancy's magic screen
   Forms of the pure and bright.

Smile on, smile on, though vain the wish,
   May'st thou for aye, as now,
Unsullied keep the stamp of truth
   Upon thine open brow,
Still may the joyous laugh speak out
   Unclouded from thine eyes,
Till Heaven reclaims its errant guest,
   And takes thee to the skies.

THE CHURCHES OF NEW-ENGLAND.

BY THE REV. EZRA STILES, D. D.*

Let the great errand into America never be forgotten. Let our children be made well acquainted, among other parts of sacred history, with the history of the Hebrew nation ; in which they will see examples of public reward and public chastisement of providence in a very striking light. From the ancient example let our churches be warned, very carefully to avoid the two capital errors which proved the ruin of the Hebrew republic, and which will never fail eventually to subvert the best constituted empire—I mean *corruption* in religion and the publie virtue ; and *disunions.*

I have observed that our churches, in a distinguished sense from almost all the protestant world are founded on the Bible. Our worthy and venerable ancestors, (be their memories dear to posterity) did not, like other protestant patrons, form a system of what they thought and judged to be the true sense of revelation, and establish this for the truth ; no—it was enough for them that the Bible was the inspired rule, and this they made the only rule.

*Note 2.—See Appendix.

And hence, if on examination we should find any of the received doctrines or usages among the churches, dissonant to the sacred oracles,—if we only *judge* so,—if this on deliberation be our opinion, we may freely enjoy and profess our judgment and oppose such doctrines or customs by alleging from the scriptures only ; without appealing to human tests of divine truth, or encountering the civil and ecclesiastical hostilities with which they have been too generally enforced.

The present bounds of New England, the greater part of which is yet a wilderness, permit an increase of seven millions. If Providence should complete the reduction of Canada and an honorable peace annex it to the British crown, we may extend our settlements into new provinces, or to the western part of those provinces which by the charters cross the continent to the Pacific ocean. With pleasure we anticipate the rapid settlement of new towns and provinces around us, and filling them up with millions of inhabitants. We transport ourselves to the distance of a hundred years forward, look over the wide spread wilderness, see it blossom like the rose, and behold it planted with churches and temples consecrated to the pure worship of the most High—when our present plain edifices shall be succeeded with a nobler species of building not indeed with temples whose colonades are decked with the gilt busts of angels winged ; but temples adorned with all the decent ornaments of the most sublime and august architecture—when divinely resplendent truth shall triumph, and our brethren of the congregational communion may form a body of seven millions! A glorious and respectable body this, for Truth and Liberty. Well might our fathers die with pleasure, and sacrifice their lives with joy to lay the foundation of such a name, of such a peculiar people whose numbers so soon increase like the sand of the sea, or the stars of heaven, and what is more, whose God is the Lord.

1760.

"MAN WAS" NOT "MADE TO MOURN."

BY THOMAS C. HARTSHORN.

Tune to joy the sprightly measure,
  Utter not a note of woe,
Give a loose to mirth and pleasure,
  Bid the generous feeling flow.
Lo! the bounties of creation
  To whatever side we turn,
Still convey this intimation,
  Man was never made to mourn.

Flowers that deck the earth with glory,
  Birds that warble in the grove,
Tell the same unvaried story
  Of our great Creator's love.
This should clear the heart of sadness
  And to pure devotion raise,
Sorrow is ungrateful madness,
  Cheerfulness is silent praise.

Though the clouds of dark despair
  Often gather round the soul,
Mirth should scatter them in air
  And dispense its sweet control.
While the bounteous hand of Heaven
  Pours its gifts from plenty's horn,
Though some transient ties are riven,
  Grateful hearts should briefly mourn.

PLAN FOR A NATIONAL UNIVERSITY.

BY THE HON. ASHER ROBBINS.

An Institution, I conceive, may be devised, of which, at present there is no model either in this country or in Europe; giving such a course of education and discipline as would give to the faculties of the human mind an improvement and power far beyond what they obtain by the ordinary systems of education; and far beyond what they afterwards attain in any of the professional pursuits. Such an Institution, as to its principle, suggested itself to the sagacious and far-seeing mind of Bacon, as one of the greatest importance. But while his other suggestions have been followed out with such wonderful success in extending the boundaries of physical science, this has been overlooked and neglected. One reason is, that the other suggestions were more elaborately explained by him; there, too, he not only pointed out the path, but he led the way in it himself. Besides, those other suggestions could be carried out by individual exertion and enterprise, independently of the existing establishments. But this required an original plan of education, and a new foundation for its execution; where the young mind would be trained by a course of education and discipline that would unfold and perfect all his faculties; where the genius would plume his young wings, and prepare himself to take the noblest flights. The idea, however, was not entirely original with Bacon; for it would be in effect but the revival of that system of education and discipline which produced such wonderful improvement and power of the human mind in Greece and Rome, and especially in Greece. Its effects here, I am persuaded, would be many and glorious. Of these I shall now indicate only one; but that one whose importance all must admit. In its progress, and ultimately, it would give to our country, I have no doubt, a national literature of a high and immortal character. However mortifying to our national pride it is to say it, it must be confessed that we have not a national literature of that character; nor is it possible we ever should have, as it appears to me, on our present systems of education. Not that our literature, such as it is, is inferior to that of other nations produced at the present day. No; mediocrity is the character of all literary works of the present day, go where you will. It is so in England, it is so in France, the two most literary nations of Europe. It is true, learned men and great scholars are every where to be found; indeed, they may be said to abound more than ever; the whole world has become a reading world; the growth of the press is prodigious; but it is all ephemeral and evanescent—all destined to the grave of oblivion. Nor is it that our countrymen have not the gift of genius for literary works of that high and immortal character. Probably no people were ever blessed with it in a greater degree—of which every where we see the indications and the evidence; but what signifies genius for an art without discipline, without knowledge of its principles and skill in that art?

> "Vis consili expers, mole ruit sua;
> Vim temperatam, Dii quoque provehunt,
> In majus."

Literature is now every where mediocre—because the arts of literature are no where cultivated, but every where neglected—and apparently despised.

The object of education is two-fold, knowledge and ability; both are important, but ability by far the most so. Knowledge is so far important as it is subsidiary to the acquiring of ability, and no further; except as a source of mental pleasure to the individual. It is ability that makes itself to be felt by society; it is ability that wields the sceptre over the human heart and the human intellect. It is a great mistake to suppose that knowledge imparts ability of course. It does indeed impart ability of a certain kind; for by exercising the attention and the memory it improves the capacity for acquiring; but the capacity to acquire is not ability to originate and produce. No; ability can only be given by the appropriate studies, accompanied with the appropriate exercises—directed by a certain rule, and conducting infallibly to a certain result.

In all the celebrated schools of Athens, this was the plan of education; and there the ingenuous youth blessed with faculties of promise, never failed to attain the eminence aspired to, unless his perseverance failed. Hence the mighty effects of those schools; hence that immense tide of great men which they poured forth on all the departments of science and letters; and especially of letters; and hence, too, the astonishing perfection of their works. A celebrated writer, filled with astonishment at the splendor as well as the number of the works preduced by the scholars of these schools, ascribes the event to the hand of a wonder-working Providence, interposed in honor of human nature, to show to what perfection the species might ascend. But there was nothing of miracle in it; the means were adequate to the end. It is no wonder at all that such schools gave to Athens her Thucydides in history, her Plato in ethics; Sophocles to her drama, and Demosthenes to her forum and her popular assemblies; and gave to her besides, that host of rivals to these and almost their equals. It was the natural and necessary effect of such a system of education; and especially with a people who held, as the Athenians did, all other human considerations as cheap in comparison with the glory of letters and the arts.

It is true, this their high and brilliant career of literary glory was but of short duration; for soon as it had attained its meridian blaze, it was suddenly arrested, for the tyrant came and laid the proud freedom of Athens in the dust, and the Athenians were a people with whom the love of glory could not survive the loss of freedom. For freedom was the breast at which that love was fed; freedom was the element in which it lived and had its being; freedom gave to it the fields where its most splendid triumphs were achieved. The genius of Athens now drooped; fell from its lofty flights down to tame mediocrity—to ephemeral works born but to languish and to die; and so remained during the long rule of that ruthless despotism—the Macedonian; and until the Roman came to put it down, and to merge Greece in the Roman Empire. Athens now was partially restored again to freedom. Her schools which had been closed, or which had existed only in form, revived with something of their former effect. They again gave forth some works worthy of her former fame, though of less transcendent merit; and they now gave to Rome the Roman eloquence and literature.

> Græcia capta serum Victorem cepet, et artes
> Intulet agresti satis:

and, if we are wise to profit by their example, may yet give to us an equal eloquence and literature.

I mention these things to show what encouragement we have to this enterprise—what well-grounded hope of success. We have only to tread the path that led the Athenian to his glory, and to open that path to the youth of our country. All the animating influences of freedom exist here in still greater force than they existed there; for, while it is not less absolute here, it is better regulated—better combined with order and security. Neither is the gift of genius wanting here; the gleams of this precious ore are seen to break out here and there all over the surface of our society; the *animus acer et sublimis* is daily displayed by our countrymen in all the forms of daring and enterprise; the Eagle, their emblem, is not more daring in his flights. And if the love of fame, which was the ruling passion of the Greek, is not now so strong with us, it is because the want of the means, the want of plain and sure directions for its pursuits, begets a despair of its attainment. The Greek had these means, had these plain and sure directions; and it was the certainty of success by perseverance and by their guide that kindled and sustained his passion and made it his ruling passion. This passion is now burning in the young bosoms of thousands of our youth; but it is, as I have said, *vis consili expers*, and struggles in vain because it struggles blindly for the fame it pants after. Let this Athenian mode of education be adopted in this instance*—let it produce but a few examples of eminent success, and thousands would rush to the path that had led to that success; and there are many among us yet young enough to see a new era arising in our land—another golden age of literature, no less splendid than any that has gone before it—not excepting even the Athenian.

OLD GRIMES.

BY ALBERT G. GREENE.

OLD Grimes is dead; that good old man
  We never shall see more :—
He used to wear a long, black coat
  All buttoned down before.

His heart was open as the day,
  His feelings all were true;
His hair was some inclined to grey,
  He wore it in a queue.

*Referring to the Smithsonian bequest.

Whene'er he heard the voice of pain,
His breast with pity burned ;
The large, round head upon his cane
From ivory was turned.

Kind words he ever had for all ;
He knew no base design :
His eyes were dark and rather small,
His nose was acquiline.

He lived at peace with all mankind,
In friendship he was true :
His coat had pocket holes behind,
His pantaloons were blue.

Unharmed, the sin which earth pollutes
He passed securely o'er,
And never wore a pair of boots
For thirty years or more.

But good old Grimes is now at rest,
Nor fears misfortunes frown :
He wore a double-breasted vest ;
The stripes ran up and down.

He modest merit sought to find,
And pay it its desert ;
He had no malice in his mind,
No ruffles on his shirt.

His neighbors he did not abuse,
Was sociable and gay ;
He wore large buckles on his shoes,
And changed them every day.

His knowledge, hid from public gaze,
He did not bring to view,—
Nor make a noise, town-meeting days,
As many people do.

His worldly goods he never threw
In trust to fortune's chances ;
But lived, (as all his brothers do,)
In easy circumstances.

Thus undisturbed by anxious cares,
His peaceful moments ran ;
And every body said he was
A fine old gentleman.

ON NOVEL WRITING.

BY MRS. JULIA CURTIS.

Although we fully appreciate the various styles of novel-writing which belong to the present age, yet, we give the preference to the smoothly told tale, which bears the impress of nature, and leads the imagination gradually on with the skill of a narrator, whose impassioned feeling is gracefully controlled. Those works which abound in passionate starts, in wild and unnatural impulses and incidental sketches of love-lorn damsels and disappointed artists, though they may possess passages of striking beauty, are infinitely less perfect than the rational, though highly wrought relations indited by greater minds.

Nor do we hesitate to assert that no other than the highest order of intellect, can produce tales resplendent with natural beauty ; for it is much easier to write a rhapsody, than a true and vivid description, and less difficult to depict the disjointed ravings of madness, than to trace the upward progress of a reasoning and philosophic mind. Any one can fancy sources of excitement which may influence the villain or the maniac ; but few can analyze the deep stirrings of the pure and high-minded, or the darker workings of the every day hypocrite. It requires an accurate knowledge of human nature, united to a keen and reflective mind, to do this ; and as few possess these properties in connexion with the imagination, requisite for the accompanying plot, such romances are rare. Greater genius is displayed in depicting the stern determination of Balfour of Burley, and the subtlety of

Rashleigh Osbaldistone, than the open villainy of Paul Clifford, or the haughty reserve of Eugene Aram. To these last novels, however, we would accord great praise. Their author is a man of brilliant thought, and admirable powers of language. But his works want nature. Human nature as it usually exists, presents a more difficult prototype for the artist, than its occasional distortions. The one requires a common imagination, the other, uncommon observation. It is with the novelist as with the landscape-painter. The latter knows that the hues of the sky and his own colors are oftentimes the same ; but to arrange his ingredients so as to present the varied and exquisite shades in nature, to blend each harmoniously with the other, so as to strike the beholder as natural, demands surpassing skill. Thus the man of lively fancy and ordinary abilities, can lay before us an imaginative tale, brilliant but inconsistent, fascinating but anomalous, a mass of possibilities, but utterly deficient in truth and discrimination. Let us not be understood, however, as advocating a suppression of the imagination for the sake of practical good sense. We consider the latter as tame and uninteresting, unattended by the former. We approve of beautiful theories and poetical dreams ; and of souls almost bursting with their proud and generous aspirations. These tend to elevate us above the stern realities of life. Though, visionary, they may be so beautifully interwoven with the coarse warp of our natures, as to give a finer character to the whole. One whose fancy thus floats along upon the severer qualities of his mind, reminds us of a bold mountain height, around the rugged outline of which, clouds of the most delicate texture are so artfully wrapt, that the whole seems softened into a heavenly shape of beauty.

We do not like those heroes and heroines, who are set apart for display, having a constant fund of difficulty to surmount ; as if it were possible to travel up and down a chain of mountains during a whole life without pausing in the vallies to take breath, and consider whether it is better to proceed or to stop short. We would rather observe the mind in this latter process, than behold it so completely wound up, that it must, ere it can stop, either break or run down. An author should relate his tale, like one who had merely observed the actions of others, and hastened to entertain his hearers with their repetition ; or "to point a moral" in the events of which he had been an eye witness. But how often in representation, men are made puppets of each other, with each string and pulley apparent to all; or, on the contrary, how often are their productions so full of plots and counterplots, that like the gordian knot, the whole must be rudely severed, or remain entangled forever.

But Scott, Cooper, James, and a few others, belong to that nobler class of writers who make the world their study, and point out the errors of the great, the virtues of the humble, the defects in human laws, and the absurdity of unnatural distinctions.

Scott deserves our thanks for the spirit he has infused into the character of his heroines in contrast with those of Cooper, who are invariably tame and insipid, acquiescent without judgment, yielding without grace, and enduring because too weak to resist. This is all wrong. A woman may approach more nearly to the general elements of the male character, without losing her identity, than is usually imagined. Allow her courage as well as fortitude, the capacity to suggest, as well as the disposition to obey, the nerve to act, as well as the power to think, and she is more perfect as a woman, provided she possesses the feminine delicacy of vision to discern the hair-line between energy and boldness, between spirit and manly daring, than she, who with a mind exclusively bent upon the preservation of the distinguishing female graces, passes a life of gentle dependence. There is a noble medium between the headlong torrent and the petty streamlet. It is the flowing river—bold but not boundless—rushing yet constrained—deep, yet not fathomless.

A woman cannot preserve her loveliness *as* a woman, unless her ambition and her love of worldly honors are subservient to the softer impulses of her heart. Shakspeare is right when he makes love control the destinies of his heroines. They may aspire reasonably, but they were never meant to trample upon their own hearts and the hearts of others for empty aggrandizement, as men may do with greater impunity. But even with men, we doubt if there are many whose ambition has not been at some time during their lives, the very slave of their affections.

It is extremely interesting to compare the different productions of our best writers with each other. Beginning with Scott, and continuing the observation down to our own Paulding, it is surprising to see what varied combinations of character are placed before us. It is as useful to give a cursory glance at this imaginary world, as it is actually to mingle with mankind in their public assemblages, or in the more refined circles. Human nature has been well sifted since the days of Fielding. He is the Shakspeare of prose. Since his bold sketches, writers have drawn more from nature than from the imagination exclusively, as formerly. It is certainly true also, that the more keenly we scan our fellow beings, the more minute do the complicated folds of their different temperaments appear. Aristotle's system of a world within a world is more true of the inward than outward nature. Enough is created; imagination need only embellish. Time is not mis-spent in perusing our best novels. We know it is the opinion of some, that when they have Shakspeare and Fielding, Milton, Johnson, &c., before them, they have enough for a life. True, here are mines of thought, but they are susceptible of numberless ramifications.

D'Israeli, in his "Curiosities of Literature," gives us a chapter upon "Imitations," which shows how much an idea may be heightened, and how gradual is its approach to perfection.

In observing how often the thoughts of others have been imbibed, unconsciously improved and re-produced by some of the greatest minds the world has ever known, we are led to believe that there is, strictly speaking nothing new under the sun. In modern days, a man of talent, is a sort of mental alchymist, and we rejoice to say, that greater success has attended the transmutation of heavy suggestions into current truths, than ever crowned the efforts of the ancient searchers for the philosopher's stone. We do not approve of too much reading. Literature should be absorbed by the mind, exactly as water is taken up by a sponge ; itself unseen, save as it increases the bulk of the original material. But to pack down the thoughts of others just as we would pack down a jar of sweetmeats, is absurd in the extreme. When the taste is once formed, then reading may be desultory. Let the compass of the mind be first extended by our acquaintanee with the solid writers, and then, every thing else will be like tributary streams, which swell the original current, while their own tiny natures are lost in its depths. Desultory reading is advantageous, because we are thus led to comprehend the full extent of our own powers. We are often in the beginning, attracted towards our best friends by a casual but happy remark. Thus may the imperfect supposition of others touch a train of thought, which afterwards embodies new and important discoveries. The mind, like the bell, is struck ere it can sound ; but the various vibrations, whether they be strong or weak, belong intrinsically to the metal of which it is composed.

PRIZE POEM.

BY SARAH H. WHITMAN.

Spoken at the opening of the Shakspeare Hall, Providence, November 27, 1838.

Hist ! what strange influence hovers in the air ?
Soft music breathes and festive torches glare,
A roseate light illumes the storied wall,
And youth and beauty throng the lofty hall ;
Lo, where the Drama, thro' the gloom of night,
Bursts in soft splendor on the ravished sight !
All hail ! bright queen of fancy's fairy train,
Long lost, long mourned, resume thy genial reign !

Can we forget when first, in childhood's hour,
Our footsteps sought thy vision-haunted bower ?
When trembling, wondering 'mid the enraptured throng,
We quaffed the tide of eloquence and song—
While stood revealed the creatures of our dream,
Bright, breathing, palpable ! scarce could we deem

That earth confessed such beauty—to abide
With *these* were life—vain shadows all beside.
O cold the hearts that from such 'witching sway
Could turn unmoved and passionless away.

But tho' less genial prove our western clime,
To Art's bright reign, than when in olden time,
Thy noblest influence filled Athena's halls,
While thundering plaudits shook her marble walls—
Yet have thy temples rose, thine altars smiled,
Where late the savage tracked the pathless wild,
And far around thy festive notes are borne,
Ere fade the echoes of the huntsman's horn.

Once more we bid thee welcome to our shores,
Confess thy empire and assert thy cause,
Again we haunt thy courts, throng round thy shrine,
And pour soft incense to the breathing Nine.

Oft when the wint'ry storms shall hurtle round,
Or silent snow-flakes print the frozen ground,
When the cold rain comes pattering on the blast,
And mantling clouds night's blazing host o'ercast,
Here shall we sit in this enchanted hall,
While "breathing thoughts and burning words" enthral,—
Regardless of the cold world's sordid strife,
And all the hollow mimicries of life—
Where vainer actors idler pageants play,
And wear their masks in the broad eye of day.

Oft shall young beauty to this shrine repair,
And manhood here cast off life's coiling care,
Entranced and spell-bound by her potent sway,
Who "calls each slumbering passion into play"—
Exulting, trembling, as her accents flow
In varying strains of triumph or of woe—
Now decked in smiles, and now her brow o'er fraught
With the pale cast of melancholy thought.

Far thro' the twilight vistas of the past,
Where gathering years their cloudy mantles cast,
Oft turns her eagle eye, and at its glance,
The shadows vanish from that drear expanse—
Lo, at her gaze night melteth into day,
And the dark mist of ages rolls away!

Each old romantic region hath she traced,
And gathered many a floweret from the waste,
Which fancy nurtured with her softest dews,
While wit and wisdom lent their golden hues.
She hath "called spirits from the vasty deep,"
Roused kings and heroes from their dreamless sleep,
Restored the scenes of a chivalrous age,
Where knightly forms heroic conflicts wage,
The victor's triumph on th' ensanguined field,
The plume, the penon, and the blazon'd shield—
Bade the dead lover's clay-cold bosom glow,
And the slain warrior meet once more his foe,

And caused them for a night on earth to roam,
Then pass like spectres to their silent home.

And now she comes with all her shadowy train
To hold her court within this gorgeous fane—
Here her bright banner fearlessly unfurls,
Nor heeds the pointless shaft the bigot hurls.
Boundless her influence, her intent sublime,
To cherish virtue and to shield from crime,
With loftiest theme to rouse the languid heart,
And stern reproof with subtle grace impart;
To wake the noble love of well earned fame,
And teach the glory of a deathless name.
She shows how heroes lived and martyrs died
And fills the exulting breast with god-like pride,
That such high energies to man are given,
To conquer earth and ope the gates of heaven.

Such themes new vigor to the heart supply,
Flush every cheek and light up every eye.

Whether in gorgeous drapery she is seen,
Moving before us like an empire's queen—
Or clothed in all the majesty of woe,
Bids beauty's tears like molten diamonds glow—
Or wreathed in smiles, with soft seducing glance,
Makes the warm life blood through the pulses dance,
Still ever beautiful she meets the sight,
Taking all shapes to furnish new delight,

Forever changing, yet forever true
To one fond aim—approving smiles from *you.*
Long may those smiles our virgin temple grace,
And SHAKSPEARE's spirit hallow all the place.

IMPOSSIBILITY OF ATHEISM.

BY THE REV. CHARLES T. BROOKS.

MEN have, in all ages and regions of the world, felt the great truth that

> "The awful shadow of some unseen power
> Floats though unseen among us."

And one who will study with a penetrating eye the heathen mythology and mysteries, will find clear traces of a belief in one God of gods running through all,—will find reason to say of heathen antiquity in general, what was so beautifully said in regard to the idolatry of Greece—

> "And yet—triumphant o'er this pompous show
> Of art, this palpable array of sense
> On every side encountered;—a *Spirit* hung
> Beautiful Region! o'er thy towns and farms,
> Statues and temples and memorial tombs."

The ancient heathen, though he knew not what he worshipped, did in reality dimly adore one Divinity.

He adored, indeed, in name and form, gods of the winds, the woods, and the waters, but it was the one, eternal, almighty, and all pervading spirit or power, which gave life and motion to the wind, the forest and the river, that he felt and reverenced. And we may discern amidst the strange and monstrous creations of the ancient heathen mythology—amidst the strong workings of the heathen mind, a tendency and an effort to make intelligible to the understanding that truth of the being of one supreme power, which has always dwelt and will always dwell in the heart and conscience of man. They bowed down, indeed, to the images of many gods, but there was a Father of gods, as well as of men, *as certain of their own poets said.* And more than this, there were the mysterious and inexorable Fates to whose eternal decrees gods as well as men were subject. The self-styled or self-fancied Atheist, though in his zeal against certain ideas of God that have darkened and degraded the human soul, he may sometimes be hurried so far as to seem to himself, as well as others, to deny Divine Providence itself,—cannot in the wildest wanderings of his spirit, fly from himself and therefore cannot escape from the presence of the Being who made him, who dwells within his body as in a temple, and numbereth the very hairs of his head. And although he may have seen so much iniquity committed in the name of the Most High, as to induce him to refuse that name a place in his system of belief, nevertheless he cannot in fact and in feeling remain "without God in the world"—in other words he cannot be actually an Atheist. If he be a man of strong feelings of justice coupled with a somewhat sombre temperament, he will see every where the footsteps of some ever-working, resistless and inexorable power, to which he may give the name of Destiny. And the decrees of this Despot, he will be ever nerving himself to bear and to defy. To him then, Fate or Necessity will be a God. If he be a man of no settled principles whatever—a mere straw on the waves of the world, then you will find him the "dark idolator of chance." He will court the caprices of a Being who is dimly imaged to his mind under the name of Fortune, and even pray to her in his heart. Or if he be one whose kindlier affections have never been polluted by sophistry or by selfishness, then, however he may declaim against the name or against some of the imputed attributes of Jehovah, his heart will go forth in love and rise in adoration to a Mother Nature—he will worship with all his faculties and feelings a mighty and mysterious power, goodness and wisdom—which he may choose to call the "Soul of the Universe." If his spiritual nature be cultivated, he will commune with this all-pervading, all-embracing, all-animating Soul in every place and season. To him the whisper of the winds, the moan of the billows and all the sounds of Nature, will be the audible voice—the universal air will be the breath—and the blue sky the serene countenance of a Being, whom though he may not choose to name him as men name him, his heart and soul and all that is within him, impel him irresistibly to love and reverence as the source and support of all creatures.

So deeply has the Creator engraven on man's heart a sense of his being and agency—so true it is—to quote a happy illustration of the thought, that as the needle touched by the loadstone, turns, after all its deviations, tremblingly faithful to the pole—so the Soul of man touched by the Holy Spirit, turns, amidst its wildest errors, tremblingly faithful to the throne of God.

PAUL PREACHING AT ATHENS.

SUGGESTED BY THE CARTOON OF RAFFAELLE.

BY ANNE C. LYNCH.

GREECE! hear that joyful sound,
A stranger's voice upon thy sacred hill,
Whose tones shall bid the slumbering nations round,
Wake with convulsive thrill.
Athenians! gather there, he brings you words
Brighter than all your boasted lore affords.

He brings you news of One
Above Olympian Jove. One in whose light
Your gods shall fade like stars before the sun;
On your bewilder'd night
That UNKNOWN GOD of whom ye darkly dream,
In all his burning radiance shall beam.

Behold, he bids you rise
From your dark worship round that idol shrine,
He points to him who rear'd your starry skies,
And bade your Phœbus shine.
Lift up your souls from where in dust ye bow,
That God of gods commands your homage now.

But, brighter tidings still!
He tells of one whose precious blood was spilt
In lavish streams upon Judea's hill,
A ransom for your guilt,—
Who triumphed o'er the grave, and broke its chain;
Who conquer'd Death and Hell, and rose again

Sages of Greece ! come near—
Spirits of daring thought and giant mould,
Ye questioners of time and nature, hear
Mysteries before untold !
Immortal life revealed ! light for which ye
Have tasked in vain your proud philosophy.

Searchers for some First Cause
Midst doubt and darkness, lo ! he points to One
Where all your vaunted reason lost must pause,
And faint to think upon.
That was from everlasting, that shall be
To everlasting still, eternally.

Ye followers of him
Who deemed his soul a spark of Deity !
Your fancies fade,—your master's dreams grow dim
To this reality.
Stoic ! unbend that brow, drink in that sound !
Skeptic ! dispel those doubts, the Truth is found.

Greece ! though thy sculptured walls
Have with thy triumphs and thy glories rung,
And through thy temples and thy pillar'd halls,
Immortal poets sung,—
No sounds like these have rent your startled air,
They open realms of light and bid you enter there.

ON THE REMOVAL OF THE REMAINS OF WASHINGTON.

BY THE HON. TRISTAM BURGES.

On the 13th of February, 1832, a Resolution was introduced into the House of Representatives, to remove the remains of Washington from Virginia, and to place them in a vault under the centre of the Capitol.

If I look back towards the beginning of life, memory is in a moment filled with bright and joyous recollections of that time, when even in the distant and humble neighborhood of my birth, the lessons of youth, and of childhood, when the very songs of the cradle were the deeds, the glory, the praises of Washington.

Think you, these teachings have ceased in the land; that these feelings are dead in our country?

Cannot we, who regard the buried remains of the great Father of our Country, as the earthly remains of no other mortal man are regarded; cannot we, awed and subdued with gratitude, with more than filial piety; cannot we approach the hallowed repository, and roll back the stone from the door of the sepulchre, without the guilt of sacrilege? Cannot his country remove the remains of this, its great Founder; and carry them in solemn procession, accompanied by all the rights of religion, and all the sanctity of its ministers; and finally deposite them in the national cemetry provided for that purpose under the foundation of this building,* which thenceforth shall be, not only the temple of freedom, legislation, and justice, but also the august mausoleum of Washington? Who, of all the civilized world, will, while these reverential movements are performing, who will point his finger at these solemnities, and call them a mere pageant?

It is the feeling, the purpose of the persons, and not the place or the subject which renders their deed pious or profane. Can we never again without sacrilege, look into the dark house of those so dear to us, until they, bursting the cerements of the tomb, are clothed with immortality? How often does the piety of children, how often the anxious affection of parents, induce them to remove the remains of endeared relatives, to places of more appropriate sepulture? How often do nations remove to their own countries, from distant foreign lands, the bones of their illustrious dead? Was it sacrilege in the Hebrews, when migrating from Egypt, to take from

*The Capitol at Washington.

the consecrated catacomb or pyramid, where for centuries they had been deposited, the bones of the illustrious founder of one of their families, and the preserver of them all ; and bearing them from the populous valley of the Nile, the learned and luxurious realm of the Pharaoh's, the scene of all his glory that they might carry them to a land of rocks and mountains ; and render his burial place one of the eternal monuments of their country? So it has continued ; and at this day it is, by the dwellers on the hill or on the plain, pointed out to the traveller as the tomb of Joseph the Patriarch.

We are told that the last will and testament of Washington, points out the place and directs the manner of his interment ; and if we remove his bones from their present repository, we shall violate that will, and set at defiance principles dear to all civilized nations. Did indeed, then, this great man prohibit this people from doing honor to his remains by placing them in a mausoleum more suitable to his illustrious life, and to the gratitude of Americans? He, like all Christian men, directed by his last will, that his body should have Christian burial ; and prescribed the manner, he selected the place for that purpose. How shall we expound that will? It has been expounded for us ; and that too, by one, who was the partner of his perils and triumphs, his labors and councils. One, who shared with him all life could give—and stood by him in the hour of dissolution. Think you, that she would have violated his will ; and that too in the beginning of her bereavement ; in the first dark hours of her earthly desolation? "Taught by his great example," she gave up those remains at the call of her country.

I cannot join in the pious incantation of those who would, in imagination, call up the mighty dead, and put them to inquisition, concerning these obsequies. Who, if he might, would bring back from the blessedness of heaven, to the cares of earth, one purified spirit ; or for a moment interrupt the felicities of those realms of reality, by any thing which agitates human feelings, in this region of dust and shadows? Permit me to learn from his life, what his country may, with propriety, do with his remains, after his death. When that immortal soul, now as we trust in beatitude, inhabited and animated his mortal part, where was the place, what was the service to which the voice of his country called him, and he was not there? In the toils of war, in the councils of peace, he was, soul and body devoted to that people, whom he labored through life to build up into one great nation. Should that body at this time be less at the service of his country, than when alive, with the imperishable soul it was, Washington, and walked the world, for human welfare ? If his whole life doth tell us, that he placed himself at the call of his country, then truly where should all that remains, be finally found, but where the same voice would place them ?

We would not raise over him "a pyramid, a monument, like the eternal mountains." No, the folly of ancient ambition, has perished from the earth, while these its monuments still stand unmoved upon its surface. This House, we trust will endure as long as this nation endures. Let this be the Mausoleum of Washington. We would place his remains in the cemetery built for that purpose, under the centre of that dome which covers the Rotunda. Directly over this on that floor, we would erect a pedestrian statue of that man, sufficiently colossal, and placed on a pedestal so high and massy, as might be required to fill and satisfy the eye, in the centre of that broad and lofty room, which, probably, has no equal in the architecture of the world.

The ever-during marble will give to coming generations the form and the features of Washington; and the traveller of future ages shall learn where he may find his tomb. This House, this Mausoleum of one, who prospered by Divine assistance, performed more for his country and for the human race, than any other mortal, shall be a place of pilgrimage for all nations. Hither will come the brave, the wise, the good, from every part of our country; not to worship, but to stand by the sepulchre and to relume the light of patriotism at the monument of Washington.

A DAY OF THE INDIAN SUMMER.

BY SARAH H. WHITMAN.

"Yet one more smile, departing distant sun
Ere o'er the frozen earth the loud winds run
And snows are sifted o'er the meadows bare."—*Bryant.*

A DAY of golden beauty!—Through the night
The hoar-frost gathered o'er each leaf and spray
Weaving its filmy network, thin and bright
And shimmering like silver in the ray
Of the soft, sunny morning—turf and tree
Pranct in its delicate embroidery,
And every withered stump and mossy stone,
With gems encrusted and with seed-pearl sown;
While in the hedge the frosted berries glow,
The scarlet holly and the purple sloe,

And all is gorgeous, fairy-like and frail
As the famed gardens of the Arabian tale.

How soft and still the varied landscape lies,
Calmly outspread beneath the smiling skies,
As if the earth in prodigal array
Of gems and broidered robes kept holiday ;
Her harvest yielded and her work all done
Basking in beauty 'neath the autumn sun !

Yet once more through the soft and balmy day
Up the brown hill-side, o'er the sunny brae
Far let us rove—or, through lone solitudes
Where "autumn's smile beams through the yellow woods,"
Fondly retracing each sweet, summer haunt
And sylvan pathway—where the sunbeams slant
Through yonder copse, tinging the saffron stars
Of the witch-hazel with their golden bars,
Or, lingering down this dim and shadowy lane
Where still the damp sod wears an emerald stain,
Though ripe brown nuts hang clustering in the hedge
And the rude barberry o'er yon rocky ledge
Droops with its pendant corals. When the showers
Of April clothed this winding path with flowers,
Here oft we sought the violet, as it lay
Buried in beds of moss and lichens grey ;
And still the aster greets us as we pass
With her faint smile—among the withered grass

Beside the way, lingering as loth of heart,
Like me, from these sweet solitudes to part.

Now seek we the dank borders of the stream
Where the tall fern-tufts shed a ruby gleam
Over the water from their crimsoned plumes,
And clustering near the modest gentian blooms
Lonely around—hallowed by sweetest song,
The last and loveliest of the floral throng.
Yet here we may not linger, for behold,
Where the stream widens, like a sea of gold
Outspreading far before us—all around
Steep wooded heights and sloping uplands bound
The sheltered scene—along the distant shore
Through colored woods the glinting sunbeams pour,
Touching their foliage with a thousand shades
And hues of beauty, as the red light fades
Upon the hill-side 'neath yon floating shroud,
Or, from the silvery edges of the cloud
Pours down a brighter gleam. Gray willows lave
Their pendant branches in the crystal wave,
And slender birch-trees o'er its banks incline,
Whose tall, slight stems across the water shine
Like shafts of silver—there the tawny elm,
The fairest subject of the sylvan realm,
The tufted pine-tree and the cedar dark,
And the young chestnut, its smooth polished bark
Gleaming like porphyry in the yellow light,
The dark brown oak and the rich maple dight

In robes of scarlet, all are standing there
So still, so calm in the soft misty air
That not a leaf is stirring—nor a sound
Startles the deep repose that broods around,
Save when the robin's melancholy song
Is heard from yonder coppice, and along
The sunny side of that low, moss-grown wall
That skirts our path, the cricket's chirping call,
Or, the fond murmur of the drowsy bee
O'er some lone flowret on the sunny lea,
And, heard at intervals, a pattering sound
Of ripened acorns rustling to the ground
Through the crisp, withered leaves.—How lonely all,
How calmly beautiful! Long shadows fall
More darkly o'er the wave as day declines,
Yet from the west a deeper glory shines,
While every crested hill and rocky height
Each moment varies in the kindling light
To some new form of beauty—changing through
All shades and colors of the rainbow's hue,
" The last still loveliest" till the gorgeous day
Melts in a flood of golden light away,
And all is o'er. Before to-morrow's sun
Cold winds may rise and shrouding shadows dun
Obscure the scene—yet shall these fading hues
And fleeting forms their loveliness transfuse
Into the mind—and memory shall burn
The painting in on her enamelled urn

In undecaying colors. When the blast
Rages around and snows are gathering fast,
When musing sadly by the twilight hearth
Or lonely wandering through life's crowded path
Its quiet beauty rising through the gloom
Shall soothe the languid spirits and illume
The drooping fancy—winning back the soul
To cheerful thoughts through nature's sweet control.

THE PRESENT INTELLECTUAL AND POLITICAL CONDITION OF EUROPE.

BY THE REV. FRANCIS WAYLAND, D. D.

Within the last fifty years, the intellectual character of the middling and lower classes of society throughout the civilized world has materially improved, and the process of improvement is at present going forward with accelerated rapidity. A taste for that sort of reading, which requires considerable reflection, and even some acquaintance with the abstract sciences, is every day becoming more widely disseminated. And not only is the number of newspapers multiplying beyond any former precedent, but it is found necessary to enlist in their service a far greater portion of literary talent than at any other period.

And truth obliges us to state, that this melioration owes much of its late advancement to the pious zeal of Protestant Christians. Desirous to extend the means of salvation to the whole human race, these benevolent men have labored with perseverance and success, not only to circulate the Bible, but to enable men to read it. Hence have arisen the British and Foreign Bible Society, the British and Foreign School Society, the Baptist Irish Society, the multiplied free schools, and the innumerable Sabbath Schools, which are so peculiarly the glory of the present age of the church. And surely it is delightful to witness the disciples of Him, who went about doing good, thus girding themselves to the work of redeeming their fellow men from ignorance and sin. O! it is a goodly thing to behold the rich man pouring forth from his abundance, and the poor man casting in his mite; the old man directing by counsel, and the young man seconding him by exertion; the matron visiting the prison, and the young woman instructing the Sabbath School; and all pledging themselves, each one to the other, that, God helping them, this world shall be the better for their having lived in it. The effects of these exertions are every year becoming more distinctly visible. In a short time, if the church be faithful to herself, and faithful to her God, what are now called the lower classes of society will cease to exist; men and women will be reading and thinking beings; and the word *canaille* will no longer be applied to any portion of the human race, within the limits of civilization.

In connexion with these facts, we would remark, that in consequence of this general diffusion of intelligence, nations are becoming vastly better acquainted with the physical, moral and political conditions of each other. Whatever of any moment is transacted in the legislative assemblies of one country, is now very soon known, not merely to the rulers, but also to the people of every other country. Nay, an interesting occurrence of any nature cannot transpire in an insignificant town of Europe or America, without finding its way, through the medium of the daily journals, to the eyes and ears of all Christendom. Every man must be, in a considerable degree, a spectator of the doings of the world, or he is soon very far in the rear of the intelligence of the day. Indeed, he has only to read a respectable newspaper, and he may be informed of the discoveries in the arts, the discussions in the senates, and the bearings of public opinion, all over the world.

The reasons for all this, as we have intimated, may be found chiefly in that increased desire of information, which characterizes the mass of society in the present age. Intelligence of every kind, and especially political intelligence, has become an article of profit; and, when once this is the case, there can be no doubt that it will be abundantly supplied. Beside this, it is important to remark, that the art of navigation has been within a few years materially improved, and commercial relations have become vastly more extensive. The establishment of packet ships between the two continents has brought London and Paris as near to us as Pittsburg and New-Orleans. There is every reason to believe, that, within the next half century, steam navigation will render the communication between the ports of Europe and America as frequent, and almost as regular, as that by ordinary mails. The commercial houses of every nation are establishing their agencies in the principal cities of every other nation, and thus binding together the people by every tie of interest; while at the same time they are furnishing innumerable channels, by which information may be circulated among every class of the community.

Hence it is that the moral influence, which nations are exerting upon each other, is greater than it has been at any antecedent period in the history of the world. The institutions of one country, are becoming known, almost of necessity, to every other country. Knowledge provokes to comparison, and comparison leads to reflection. The fact that others are happier than themselves, prompts men to inquire whence this difference proceeds, and how their own melioration may be accomplished. By simply looking upon a free people, an oppressive people instinctively feel that they have inalienable rights; and they will never afterwards be at rest, until the enjoyment of these rights is guaranteed to them. Thus one form of government, which in any preeminent degree promotes the happiness of man, is gradually disseminating the principles of its constitution, and from the very fact of its existence, calling into being those trains of thought, which must in the end revolutionize every government, within the sphere of its influence, under which the people are oppressed.

And thus is it that the field in which mind may labor, has now become wide as the limits of civilization. A doctrine advanced by one man, if it have any claim to interest, is soon known to every other man. The movement of one intellect, now sets in motion the intellects of millions. We may now calculate upon effects, not upon a state or a people, but upon the melting, amalgamating mass of human nature. Man is now the instrument which genius wields at its will; it touches a chord of the human heart, and nations vibrate in unison. And thus he who can rivet the attention of a community upon an elementary principle hitherto neglected in politics or in morals, or who can bring an acknowledged principle to bear upon an existing abuse, may, by his own intellectual might, with only the assistance of the press, transform the institutions of an empire or a world.

In many respects, the nations of Christendom collectively are becoming somewhat analogous to our own Federal Republic. Antiquated distinctions are passing away, and local animosities are subsiding. The common people of different countries are knowing each other better, esteeming each other more, and attaching themselves to each other by various manifestations of reciprocal good will. It is true, every nation has still its separate boundaries and its individual interests; but the freedom of commercial intercourse is allowing those interests to adjust themselves to each other, and thus rendering the causes of collision of vastly less frequent occurrence. Local questions are becoming of less, and general questions of greater importance. Thanks be to God, men have at last begun to understand the rights, and to feel for the wrongs, of each other. Mountains interposed do not so much make enemies of nations. Let the trumpet of alarm be sounded, and its notes are now heard by every nation whether of Europe or America. Let a voice borne on the feeblest breeze tell that the rights of man are in danger, and it floats over valley and mountain, across continent and ocean, until it has vibrated on the ear of the remotest dweller in Christendom. Let the arm of oppression be raised to crush the feeblest nation on earth, and there will be heard every where, if not the shout of defiance, at least the deep-toned murmur of implacable displeasure. It is the cry of aggrieved, insulted, much-abused man. It is human nature waking in her might from the slumber of ages, shaking herself from the dust of antiquated institutions, girding herself for the combat, and going forth conquering and to conquer ; and wo unto the man, wo unto the dynasty, wo unto the party, and wo unto the policy, on whom shall fall the scath of her blighting indignation.

That two parties are forming in every country,

we have abundant evidence; it is equally evident that the question on which they are divided is of the utmost magnitude; and that it is, in every nation, substantially the same.

As to their present state, we may observe, that the one has enlisted the greatest numbers, while the other wields the most effective force. The one comprises the lower and middling classes of society, which are of course by far the most numerous, and the other, the rulers and their immediate dependants. The physical power of any nation always resides with the governed, and it is the governed who are the friends of free institutions. But it is to be remarked, that the millions who desire reform are scattered abroad over our immense tracts of country, each one by his own fireside, without concert, and destitute of the means for organized operation; on the contrary, the force of the rulers is always collected, and can at any moment be brought to bear upon any portion of territory, in which there might appear the least movement towards revolution.

But the friends of popular institutions are opposed, in every nation, by more than the force of their own rulers. Whilst they are powerful only at home, the rulers are able to bring all their forces to bear upon a single point in any part of the civilized world.

To accomplish this purpose, seems the principal design of the Holy Alliance ; and hence they have pledged the physical force of the whole to each other, whenever a question shall be agitated in any country, on which depends the rights of the people.

If we compare their prospects, we shall find that the popular party is increasing with amazing rapidity. Nations are already flocking to its standard. Fifty years ago, and it could be hardly said to exist, only as the voice of indignant freemen was heard in yonder hall,* the far famed "cradle of liberty." From that moment, its progress has been right onward. A continent has since declared itself free. In the old world, the principles of liberty are becoming more universally received, more thoroughly understood, and more ably supported. Education is becoming every day more widely disseminated; and every man, as he learns to think, ranks himself with the friends of intellectual improvement. The trains of thought are already at work, which must effect important modifications in the social edifice, or that edifice, undermined from its foundations, must crumble into ruin.

And thus, from these very causes, the other party is rapidly declining. Nations are leaving it. The

* Faneuil Hall.

people are loathing it. It cannot ultimately succeed, until it has changed the ordinances of heaven. It cannot prosper, unless it can check that tendency to improvement, with which God endowed man at the first moment of his creation. Every report of oppression weakens it. Every Sabbath School, every Bible Society, nay, every mode of circulating knowledge weakens it. And thus, unless by some combined and convulsive effort it should for a little while recover its power, it may almost be expected that within the present age, it will fall before the resistless march of public opinion.

"WHERE IS THY BROTHER?"

BY SARAH S. JACOBS.

THERE were sounds of peace and joyousness,
In that New England place ;
And there was many a merry smile
On many a merry face ;
And the great sun went riding up,
And the broad river ran ;
All things seemed hideously glad
To me a guilty man.

I could not bear the yellow light
As it streamed so pure and clear ;

The holy look of the village church,
  It thrilled me thro' with fear.
I turned away from the gentle stream,
  And from the smiling land,
For their peace was torture unto one
  With blood upon his hand.

I saw the city's distant spires,
  I saw the old turrets gray,
And the household chimneys and the smoke
  With the fresh air at play.
I loathed them all, they mocked me so,
  They would not let me be,
But still kept pointing to the heaven
  That I might never see.

As the sun-shine chasëd the sportive cloud
  O'er the fields of golden grain,
The darker fell and heavier,
  The cloud upon my brain.
The shadow of the broad old oak
  Slanted to reach his grave ;
And the river told the sky my crime
  In the blood tint of its wave.

The trees in the wood towered loftier,
  Their outlines grew harsh and grim,
And they seemed to struggle hard with me,
  As I had striven with him.
A deadly shudder crept o'er the world,

Tho' the sun shone pleasantly,
And I knew that the eyes of the buried man,
Were peeping out at me.

The innocent flowers beside my path
Looked pale and shivering ;
Oh ! the whole earth was cursed for me,
The only guilty thing.
The blessed beauty of a child,
With its lovely eyes and hair ;
I thought it would cool my fevered heart,
Oh God ! *his* smile was there.

I shrunk away from his wondering look
From his gentle hand away ;
"Oh ! come with me," he cried, "or else
You'll be too late to pray."
For the bells were tolling in the tower ;
And in the stillness calm,
Unbroken to the ear of heaven
Rung out the morning psalm.

The pleasant child looked back at me,
And shut the church-yard gate ;
Alas ! I knew as he had said
It was indeed *too late.*
And then I sat down quietly,
Despair had made me strong ;
It passed in tearless suffering,
That lonely day and long.

The sun had watched me close all day,
  And when his beams were low
Men came and in the pleasant fields,
  Were walking to and fro.
I saw one with a quiet garb
  A hat with an ample brim
And a placid look, as if the world
  Were placid unto him.

And he spoke kindly unto me
  Touched by my wretched face ;
And asked me why I sat so still
  All day in that same place ?
I told him all, I told him all,
  And others round us came ;
What cared I ? the wide universe
  Already knew my shame.

And how I loved the dead, I told
  As if he were my brother ;
And how I struck a cruel blow,
  Another, and another.
How I buried him beneath the oak,
  Two nights before, in the rain ;
And I prayed them for sweet mercy's sake,
  Not to leave me there again.

I thought not of the magistrate,
  I thought not to atone ;

I dreaded nothing but to stay
With my dead friend alone.
Then those around us went away
The kindly Quaker stayed,
He did not speak to me, but since,
I 've thought for me he prayed.

An hour or more we waited thus
The peaceful man and I,
Until the boldest of the stars
Was flashing in the sky.
And then, all sinful as I was,
Doomed to a death of shame,
The sleep I had not found before,
Cool and refreshing came.

The Quaker held my hand the while,
The tree waved o'er my head ;
One, two, to watch me, and the star
Another, and the *dead.*
So when the men came from the town
To take me to be tried,
The murdered and the murderer,
Were sleeping side by side.

THE AMERICAN REVOLUTION.

BY THE HON. ASHER ROBBINS.

There has been no revolution known in the history of mankind, so interesting in itself, for the national character it attested; so memorable in its circumstances, for the national virtues it evinced; so favorable in its consequences, directly to the people who accomplished it, and indirectly to the rest of mankind. It stands, and will forever stand, as a monument of peculiar glory to the American people; and as the guiding star of every other in their struggles for freedom. Whenever, and wherever any people, indignant at their wrongs, shall rise resolved to vindicate their rights, they will turn their eyes to this guiding star; to cheer and to animate, as well as to guide them. Our example will be their study, their model; here they will take their lessons; here they will learn how to fight the battles of freedom, and to triumph in the contest; here they will learn the more difficult lesson, how to secure and to perpetuate all the blessings of that triumph; here they will see demonstrated that the people are capable of self-government, and of a government, too, far excelling all others in security, and the blessings it bestows ; here they will find a practical refutation of the doctrines so industriously taught them by their rulers in every age, that a power independent of their own, and superior to their own, is essential to their happiness, as being essential to their security ; here they will see that the most powerful, the most prosperous, and the most happy of all governments, is the government of the people, by the people.

Such a guiding star it has already been to the liberated nations of the South on this continent. In the great resolve to achieve their freedom and independence ; in the severe conflicts of their long and sanguinary struggles ; in their institutions, and forms of government ; they have studied, have imitated, have emulated our great example ; and success has crowned their efforts. They too have their sages, and their heroes ; if they have not had a WASHINGTON, that seems a favor reserved by Providence for our peculiar felicity ; recollect that WASHINGTON stands alone ; without compeer in the ages that preceded, and probably to be without compeer in the ages that are to follow him. It is fabled that there could be but one Phœnix ; it would seem a fact that there can be but one Washington ; he stands, and probably will forever stand, at the head of human kind ; too elevated to have a rival, almost too elevated to have a second. But though they have not had the compeer of Washington, they have had, as I said, and have, their heroes and their sages who have enabled them to achieve their independence. They have now taken their equal stations with the independent nations of the earth ; with whom they have formed, and are forming their relations ; they have adopted and are adopting institutions on the model of our own ; institutions that will give full scope to all the energies of regulated freedom, operating throughout their immense regions, fertile in boundless resources. No longer the hand of a foreign domination lies there as a curse upon the land ; withering and blasting even nature herself ; that made the most fertile portions of the earth, in a manner, a barren waste ; that lay like an incubus upon the faculties of man, and benumbed like a torpedo. No ; that blasting hand, is now itself blasted, and is shaken off : Freedom now reigns there ; from the summits of their Andes, to the shores of either ocean, her banners unfurled to the breeze, float in triumphant pride ; blessing those nations, by those happy nations blessed. The Genius of our Revolution towering to the heavens, and pointing to those happy nations, may say, in pride of heart may say, "*Ecce meos filios.*"

The American people have led and are leading in the van of freedom for mankind. The march of that freedom may be slow; but there is reason to believe, it will be sure and irresistible, and that all absolute thrones will sooner or later fall before it. Already those thrones have to rely on the brute force only of the military arm; for they have lost or are fast losing their two other great props, the ignorance and the superstition of their people, by the diffusion of knowledge and of the spirit of inquiry among them. Nor is this military arm, singly for each, deemed by them a sufficient security to each; for, abjuring their mutual wars of ambition and conquest, they have leagued together for their mutual defence against their own people; and have deemed the united force of all necessary to each, against the single people of each. Now this spirit of the people, so dreaded by these thrones, takes its great force from the example of our revolution; there it feeds itself, thence it grows and becomes the ruling passion. The love of liberty is a sentiment natural to the human heart; but the want of it, though that is always felt as a severe privation, it is not felt as a reproach, so long as it is the common lot of all; and if the privation is not aggravated by outrages, it is not apt to impel to action: But if liberty has been acquired and is enjoyed by others, and the example is ever present to the view, and the results are enviable, then it is coveted; then the contrast makes the privation felt as a reproach. It is the sting of this reproach, this wounded pride, impatient of degradation, and eager to avenge itself, grafted on this innate love of freedom, that impels to action; that prompts the noble purpose, that urges the daring hand to vindicate the rights of insulted nature. Yes: insulted nature; for every arbitrary throne is an insult to nature. What greater indignity to man than to be made the property of his fellow-man; to have no share in the power that rules him; to be subject to the abuses of that power, and that power always tending to abuse; corrupted itself, and corrupting its possessor; by its own nature and necessary operation corrupting him. It is thus that the influence of our Revolution is silently undermining arbitrary thrones, and preparing their fall; it is by nourishing the spirit of liberty, by begetting and inflaming an impatience of its privation; and they must fall. Their leagues, their holy alliances, may delay, but they cannot prevent their final fall. That is; the arbitrary power must be surrendered; the people must have freedom, and that freedom must be secured to the people by their forms of government.

A FRAGMENT.

BY GEORGE R. BURRILL.

WHEN tidings to Prince Edward came
"Your little son did die;"
He donned his death weeds for the same,
And grieved most piteously.

And then to them the prince did say
God's holy will be done:
The Lord did give and take away:
I 'm yet my father's son.

But when came messengers and said
"Your *father*, he did die,"
He tore his raiment, shaved his head,
And on the ground did lie.

For seven whole days, a goodly week,
He sat him down and wept;
He could not eat, he could not speak,
And never once he slept.

Then him bespake the Lord Warrenne,
"Why grieves my liege so sore?
For fair Lord John thy heart did brenne
But for King Henry more.

"Art thou not king of fair England,
E'er since thy father died,
And do not we thy servants stand
By legient homage tied?"

Then spake King Edward, "wot ye not
I may have sons a score,
With God his grace? but 'tis my lot
Ne'er to have father more."

CONNEXION BETWEEN LOVE, POETRY, MUSIC AND DEVOTION.

BY ROWLAND G. HAZARD.

LANGUAGE in its simplest form of narration, elevates us above the brute creation, to social and intelligent beings. In the form of abstraction, it becomes an engine for the acquisition of general knowledge, and thus carries us through another stage of improvement; but one in which narrow views still predominate. It still keeps pace with our intellectual and moral advancement, and when our enlarging views pass the boundary of common, direct expressions, it becomes elevated to poetry. And this combination may, in a yet further stage of advancement, be etheralized and sublimated to the more exquisite perfection of music, which, though here but a vague and misty shadow, may yet be the first indication of what is there to be embodied in the most comprehensive, perhaps infinite emanations of truth and beauty. This progression is facilitated by the generous feelings which carry us beyond the little circle of common affairs, and particularly by those excitements which elevate us far above them ; for it is only in the farther and higher departments of thought, that we are compelled to think only in the poetic form of ideals. Hence it is, that this faculty is so often first developed, when love,

> "That feeling from the Godhead caught,
> Has won from earth each sordid thought,"

and makes us conscious of a happiness too generous and exalted, too pure and etherial, too vast for words to express. The effect of this expansive sentiment upon the modes of thought and expression, is one of the most striking illustrations of the theory we have advanced, and as such deserves a further notice.

In its most romantic, and also its most ennobling form, it is the result of all the estimable qualities which the excited imagination of the lover can combine, embodied and harmonizing in some pleasing object, which has, in some generally unknown manner, excited the first emotion. When these perfections are different from any which we are conscious of possessing within ourselves, we have no means of measuring their extent, and the imagination may expand without limit to meet its wants, or its conceptions. The superiority of mind to matter, and the greater expansibility of its qualities, indicate it as the only terrestrial object capable of exciting this hallowed emotion, and the diversity, which is a necessary element in perfecting it, is found admirably designed in the modifications of the masculine and feminine characters. This is confirmed by common observation. If these views of the romantic passion are correct, it is evident that the imagination will almost immediately have filled the measure of this ideal excellence—that it will have reached, and even gone beyond the tangible object of its adoration ; and hence, although it may still retain all that it has gained, that object must lose its power of impelling it forward in the flowery paths and bright creations to which it has introduced it. We trust that we shall not be suspected of intending any disparagement of the sex, from whose purer spirit first emanated the spark which kindled in the breast of man this etherial flame.

It is much, that woman has made us acquainted with one of the infinite tendencies of the soul, to fill the never ending expansion of which, she must be more than angel. Must this influence then be arrested and the consequent improvement cease ? Has this spirituality been awakened in the soul, only to shed a momentary gleam of romance over the realities of life ? Analogy rejects the idea ; it must serve some higher purpose. And observing the path of our progression, is it not obvious that this finite feeling may be merged in the love of that which is infinite ; and in the attributes of God find an illimitable field for expansion, where every new elevation but reveals more to admire, adore, and love ; thus forever presenting a standard of superior excellence, and forever winning us towards perfection ? There is on this account, a manifest advantage in the Deity not being present to our senses in any definite, tangible form. His power, wisdom, goodness, and every perfection, are manifested to us, only in the beauty, grandeur, and designs of his creation ; but these evidences are so obvious, so numerous and so varied, that every one may discern the qualities and combine them so as to form the precise character which will correspond to his idea of perfection, and which he can most admire, love, and adore. A beau ideal, in which increased clearness of perception will only discover new beauty, and on which he may forever expatiate, and yet not sum up all its excellencies—in which his admiration will be perpetually excited by new and delightful discovery—which will continually adapt itself to the change and enlargement of his views of perfection, and appear more beautiful and lovely, the more he contemplates it. His most exalted conceptions of excellence may here always be realized, and the mode of mind is love etheralized, love sublimated to devotion, and resting not on the fleeting shadows of a feverish imagination, but on the infinite and immutable attributes of a Being, that can never be the subject of those changes and misfortunes, the thought of which will sometimes break upon the transports of the most impassioned lover. The thought of one beloved, and with whom fancy has associated every human excellence and angelic loveliness, has often elevated the mind above criminal or ignoble conduct; and if religion had done no more than furnish us with an ideal, in which we group every perfection, she would still have done much to purify the heart, ennoble the mind, and bless and protect our race. Whether the object, with which we associate this ideal excellence, be human or divine, the effect of contemplating it will be the same in kind, though varying in degree ; the tendency in either case being to produce that elevation of soul, purity of sentiment, and refinement of feeling, which are the natural guardians of virtue. It is in this view, that we may realize the fulness of an apothegm of Madame De Stael, and perceive how much more than the mere truism is conveyed in her expression, " to love God is still to love." We again repeat, that to a mind accustomed to observe and to contemplate its advancement in this delightful progression, there can be nothing terrible in that which merely accelerates it.

The observed connexion between refined intelligence, enthusiasm, love, poetry, music and devotion, bears a striking analogy to that so often noticed by natural philosophers, between heat, light, magnetism galvanism, electricity, vitality, and the nervous fluid. An ingenious attempt,* has not long since been made to elucidate the latter, by a division of matter into two classes ; the one called common

*Ultimate Principles by Lardner, Vanuxum, &c.

matter, having the power of concreting by an attractive power; the other or etherial matter, having the property of expanding by an inherent repelling tendency. All the phenomena alluded to, and indeed all other in the material world, are referred to combinations of these two, varying as the one or the other predominates in a greater or less degree. Pursuing the analogy, we may divide our moral nature into two elements—the one having an influence to contract, and keep as within the narrow limits of gross and grovelling occupations, and to which we may ascribe all the selfish feelings, which have no higher object than physical existence, or sensual pleasure, and if unaided, in its best estate, reaching no higher elevation than mechanical reasoning,—and refer the greater refinements of reason, and the generous and exalted emotions of enthusiasm, love, poetry, music and devotion, to the predominance of a finer and purer essence, already exhibiting its infinite tendency, and destined, when freed from its connexion with the gross and sensual, to expand in the purer regions of an undefined immensity.

The calculations of avarice, and the sordid maxims of selfishness, are easily embraced in finite terms; and the language of abstraction, even when directed to more ennobling pursuits, has a constant tendency to narrow the path of our advancement, and lead us to subtle, rather than improving results. The processes of ideality, on the other hand, are constantly widening and giving us more expanded views. We would therefore suggest, that the latent connexion which exists between the purer feeling and sentiments, arises from their all flowing from this source, and the property, which they consequently have of gratifying our desire for the infinite. * * *

Observation is the first faculty brought into action, and is for a time a sufficient source of mental excitement. The child is pleased with every novelty ; we may see him sound his rattle, pause, and shake it again, to assure himself that it is the effect of his own volitions, and is thus continually exhilarated by the acquisition of knowledge, and the discovery and exertion of his own powers. His store of facts accumulates, the circle around him is culled, and hence a necessity for classification and invention (the two earliest stages of reasoning and imagining) is at once produced. These enable him to reduce his particulars, and to form new combinations of them. His mind expands until these appear too limited, and reason begins to form universal propositions which are among the earliest indications of its infinite tendency. These, however, relating only to things in themselves finite, fail to meet the wants of his opening soul. The infinite begins to claim his attention. He fixes upon the most expansive of terrestrial objects, upon mind, but in a form so differing from his own, that he may conceive of it as imbued with qualities far surpassing any which he is conscious of possessing, and yet not feel himself comparatively degraded in his division of the species. This, as we have before explained, forms the poetic stage of his advancement. The finer feelings of his nature are now developed and expand themselves with a rapidity proportioned to the vast range here opened to their exercise, until even this fails to meet their wants. The universal mind alone remains ; and here all the infinite tendencies of the soul now expand themselves ; here refined intelligence, enthusiasm, love, poetry, and devotion, are united in a delightful harmony, blended in one heaven of feeling. The religious sentiment is thus fully developed by this union of all the pure and infinite tendencies of the soul, which traversing the finite, find no other sphere sufficiently comprehensive for their full developement, and nothing which harmonizes with their nature, but the manifestations and the attributes of the Godhead. In this combination, the etherial principle largely predominates, and the expansive tendency becomes so strong, that neither human force, nor human ingenuity, has yet been able to control it. It has been loaded with the chains of tyranny. It has been retarded and shackled by creeds. It has been diverted from its proper objects by cunningly devised forms, and gorgeous and imposing ceremonies. It has been wickedly directed to inexplicable mysteries, and wasted in the vain endeavor to elicit truth from terms which contained no meaning. But in despite of all these obstacles, it has advanced. It has set at defiance the power of princes, and broken the fetters they imposed. It has put at nought the subtlety of priests, and with the energy of enthusiasm penetrated beyond the forms and mysteries by which they have sought to conceal truth, and proclaimed its discoveries from the flames which surrounded it with glory, and shed lustre on its revelations. The only mode of preventing the development of this expansive principle, is by destroying some of its elements or by taking away some of the steps which are essential to its progress.

The experiment of shackling the mind with prohibitions, preventing the acquisition of knowledge, and restraining the reasoning faculties, has in part succeeded. But the step thus removed, is too short to leave an impassible barrier. The mind gets over the abhorred vacuum, and its weakened energies expand beyond it. It is by removing the next, and greater element, of our advancement, by destroying the influence of woman on society, and with it the generous emotions, the exalting influence of love, that the progress of mankind has been most effectually checked. It is where the female character is so degraded, that its etherial influence is no longer felt, that this sign of divinity has failed to exhibit itself—where from infancy man has been taught to look upon woman as a soulless toy, and woman to act as if unconscious of a higher destiny. The same effect has been elsewhere produced by her exclusion from society, and resorting to physical deformity of a kind producing sloth of body, dependence and a consequent want of mental energy. Restore the soul of woman, and the Mahometans would soon have a better, and a brighter revelation. Suffer the feet of Chinese women to grow, and the men could not long retain their grovelling, slavish dispositions, nor the government, its narrow and exclusive policy.

It is worthy of remark, that a religion adapted to the wants of the etherial nature, must, like it, possess a susceptibility to never ending expansion. It must continually exhibit higher and better state of existence than that to which we have arrived; and consequently the professors of such a religion will always be manifestly short of its teachings, while the professors of a rigid finite system of ethics may fulfil every tittle of their law. The Christian dispensation certainly appears to possess this wonderful adaptation. Its broad principles include the whole duty of man, and apply in every stage of his progression. Like the source from whence they emanate, they always fill our views of perfection. It were to be wished, that the remarks which we have just made, would account for all the acknowledged defalcations of those who profess to be the followers of its great founder. How delightful would it be to draw at once an illustration and a confirmation from such a source. How encouraging to believe, that we had improved and were still improving, though the horizon of perfection recedes as we advance. We fear, however, that we must look to other causes, for at least a portion of the disparity between the profession and practice of Christians.

STANZAS.

BY ALBERT G. GREENE.

OH think not that the bosom's light
  Must dimly shine, its fire be low,
Because it doth not all invite
  To feel its warmth and share its glow.
The altar's strong and steady blaze
  On all around may coldly shine,
But only genial warmth conveys
  To those who gather near the shrine.
The lamp within the festal hall
  Doth not more clear and brightly burn,
Than that, which shrouded by the pall,
  Lights but the cold funereal urn.

The fire which lives through one brief hour,
  More sudden heat perchance reveals,
Than that, whose tenfold strength and power
  Its own unmeasured depth conceals.
Brightly the summer cloud may glide
  But bear no heat within its breast,
Though all its gorgeous folds are dyed
  In the full glories of the West:
'T is that which through the darkened sky,
  Surrounded by no radiance, sweeps,
In which, concealed from every eye,
  The wild and vivid lightning sleeps.

Do the dull flint, the rigid steel,
  Which thou within thy hand may'st hold,
Unto thy sight or touch reveal
  The hidden power which they enfold?
But take those cold, unyielding things,
  And beat their edges till you tire,—
And every atom forth that springs,
  Is a bright spark of living fire:
Each particle, so dull and cold
  Until the blow that woke it came,
Did still within it slumbering hold
  A power to wrap the world in flame.

What is there, when thy sight is turned
  To the volcano's icy crest,
By which the fire can be discerned
  That rages in its silent breast;
Which hidden deep, but quenchless still,
  Is at its work of sure decay,
And will not cease to burn, until
  It wears its giant heart away.
The mountain's side upholds in pride
  Its head amid the realms of snow,
And gives its bosom depth to hide
  The burning mass which lies below.

While thus in things of sense alone,
  Such truths from sense lie still concealed,
How can the living heart be known,

Its secret, inmost depths revealed.
Oh, many an overburdened soul
Has been at last to madness wrought,
While proudly struggling to control
Its burning and consuming thought;
When it had sought communion long,
And had been doomed in vain to seek,
For feelings far too deep and strong
For heart to bear or tongue to speak.

RHODE-ISLAND DURING THE REVOLUTION.

BY THE HON. WILLIAM HUNTER.

The first blows struck in our Revolution in an obscure village of a remote, and almost unknown country, seem to have been heard all over the world. The inhabitants of Europe seemed roused as from the trance of ages, and soon from anxious spectators, became generous and animated actors. We had as our friends, and fellow combatants, the patriotic and chivalrous spirits of Poland—Pulaski and Kosciusko. The gallant and accomplished Fersen, of Sweden. The tacticians and disciplinarians of Austria and Prussia, De Kalb and Steuben. We mustered in our train the flower of the French nobility. The mind of Europe was with us; and we received from every philosopher, poet, or patriot of the day, cheerings of gratulation. They wept at our disasters, they rejoiced in our victories. They felt it as their own triumph, when, for the first time in the annals of man, the parent and the sovereign power acknowledged by the treaty of 1783, the rightful independence of the reproached, rebellious child, and the rightful establishment, in full sovereignty, of a new empire.

But let ns withdraw our dazzled gaze from the extended epic painting of National glory and prowess crowded with personages, lighted by the volcanic blaze of battles, and shaded by darkening clouds of sorrow and disaster, and look with endeared emotions of tenderness and love, at the MINIATURE of the parent state.

Men of Rhode Island, you are the descendants of those who were twice pilgrims ; the descendants of the victims of a double persecution. This fact of your origin has shaped your whole political character, influenced all your political movements, from the time of your feeble association, in the depths of the forests of this then houseless land, to the present moment ; and may God grant it always may so influence, and direct you. You are the descendants, equally with those who take pride from this descent, of those puritans and independents, who fled from religious persecution in England, in the hope of enjoying religious freedom here. Why your forefathers did not, could not, enjoy it, is a dark passage in the history of a sister state, which we would gladly expunge, if it were not a record necessary to prove your genealogy and birthright.

The basis of your political institution, was not merely toleration, but a perfect freedom in matters of religious concernment. No nice exceptions, no insulting indulgencies, which, while they allow the exercise of voluntary worship, deny the right, and pretend to confer a favor—deface the consistent beauty of our plan. Every aspirant to Almighty favor, in the sincerity of his devotion, has a perfect, unobstructed, inobstructible right, to seek it in the way he thinks fit. He may choose the simplest or the richest form. He may drink the waters of life, in rude simplicity, from the palm of his hand, from the crystal cup of reformed episcopacy, or from the embossed and enchased golden chalice of papal gorgeousness. Your ancestors announced this opinion and enjoyed its legal exercise, long before the able and amiable Roman Catholic Lord Baltimore, or the sagacious and benevolent Quaker William Penn, adopted and enforced it. In this great discovery, you have the incontestible merit of priority. This is a glory of which you cannot be robbed, a glory which no historian dare pass by unnoticed ; though he may be born in a land which reluctantly eulogizes, what it secretly evinces, the proud pre-eminence in effectuating that, which has contributed to the repose and felicity of mankind, more than any other discovery or declaration ; saving that of the Gospel, whence it was borrowed, and from which it necessarily results. For we have its clear authority for the assertion, that "where the spirit of the Lord is, there is Liberty,"—and that his service is perfect freedom. This freedom is not only unconquerable, but it must conquer. Opposition to it makes martyrs, but never slaves.

Where this principle is, there is a largeness of thought, a loftiness of conception, that naturally breaks the way, and opens the avenues to political rights and enjoyments. Wherever this freedom exists, political freedom co-exists. This is not too broad a position, but at any rate fearless of contradiction, we may assert that civil and political liberty, cannot be long securely maintained, without religious freedom. What man can deem himself free, when in the primary concern and consolation of his present, and the hopes and fears of his future existence, he is shackled by authority, debarred from light, and taught to shrink from a vagrant uprising thought of non-comformity to the prescribed creed, as blasphemy and enmity towards God ? Political Freedom, with cautious, not with timid step, though with her person half concealed, and the brightness of her glory veiled, attended in the train of the protestant Reformation in Europe. In the North American Colonies, she marched with a fearless and defying tread and bearing, and, with a voice sometimes loud and dread, sometimes soft and composed, scattered dismay over her foes, or breathed hope and condolence to her votaries ; because her way was opened by her pioneer—because she was strengthened, sustained, and invincibly secured, by her heaven-born sister, religious freedom.

You never would have been, you never could have been, what you have been, and what you politically are, unless for the principles of religious, always followed and accompanied by those of political freedom. They both were equally and simultaneously adopted and consecrated by your institutions. Your ancestors always had a spirit, and a daring, an original, unaccommodating character, an insurgency and elasticity of mind, which cannot otherwise be accounted for. We deny it not. We always have been in Rhode-Island reproached for heresy, both religious and political; which word heresy, being rightly interpreted, unless I have forgotten my Greek, from which language the word is derived, means the atrocious offence, of the assertion of a man's own opinion. The spirit of these remarks, emanates from our legislative history. The charter ultimately procured by the talents, address, and good fortune of Clarke, under the form of a corporation, has all the essentials of a well-tempered democracy. The king, after he granted it, virtually excluded himself from any interference with it. He had no viceroy, he had no veto on the laws of the colony. We endured not his actual or constructive presence.

We preserved the charter as the talisman of our being, the palladium of our rights, the idol of our affections. Awaiting the revolution of 1688, we temporized, and though the charter had been, so far as irregular power could do it, annulled, after that glorious event, the revolution of 1688, we went on acting under it, without clamor or apology, as unharmed and unforfeited. When the mother country was in the right, or we thought it so, nothing could surpass the energy and enthusiasm of our patriotism.

Under the fascinating influence of the administration of the elder Pitt, we sent 500 men into the Canadian expedition. We assisted, and more than in our proportion assisted, in the siege and conquest of the Havana. The truth is, that our consciousness of military merit and fortitude, was taught us by that Canadian war. We were received, and at first despised as provincials ; but we were Yankees and learnt rapidly. We frequently relieved our royal and courtly associates, from the effect of error and panic by the skill of our just taught, almost self taught officers ; and we sustained them by the unbroken fortitude, or the hardy enterprise of men, who habituated to the exercise of self opinion, and prompt in invention of all the means necessary to an end, and undaunted in their execution, knew not despair or sickness of heart. This fact is of much more importance in the history of our revolution, than has been assigned to it. We had fought by the side of British officers and soldiers, and though we did not in the result despise them, we were by no means taught to despise ourselves. This was true in a certain sense of all the colonies, but the feelings arising out of these transactions, operated much more decidedly in Rhode-Island, on account of the immense disproportion of our levies, compared to

17*

our population. This was the secret cause of our not being dismayed by the threats of regular troops, of the king's forces, of fleets, that would batter and conflagrate our towns. We were unintimidated by fulminations of devastation, and extermination. Here, in Rhode Island, we spurred on the contest. We had spirits that were solicitous to hasten events, and render battle inevitable.

Before the enactment, or during the negligent enforcement of the English Laws of Trade, we grew up with prodigious thriftiness. The new system adopted after the peace of 1763, not only checked our commerce, but indicated a systematic design of oppression. Of this design we had an intuitive conception, and to it an invincible repugnance. It has lately been stated by a British minister in the House of Commons, "that however the attempt at taxation might be viewed as the immediate cause of the American explosion, yet the train had been long laid, in the severe and unbending efforts of England to extend more rigorously than ever the Laws of Trade. "Every little case," he says, "that was brought before the Board of Trade, was treated with the utmost severity." The two really great cases that occurred, originated here. The first was the attack at Newport on the 17th

June 1769, of the armed revenue sloop Liberty, whose captain had been guilty of some oppressions and enormities. She was attacked by a band of unknown people, who cut her cables, let her drive on shore on the point, where they cut away her masts, scuttled her, carried both her boats to the recently planted Liberty Tree, at the upper end of the town, and burnt them. The second was the affair of the Gaspee on the 9th of June 1772. The first blood that was shed in the revolutionary contest, by that very act begun, stained her deck, and it was drawn by a Rhode Island hand. The blood of Lieutenant Duddington, was the first blood drawn in the American cause.

We are obliged to read in our own American books, disquisitions, almost controversial, on the question, " who gave the first impulse to the ball of the revolution," as some in degrading metaphor have chosen to express the thought. I have been compelled to listen upon this topic, to inflated declamation, rather than just argument, from grave senators, on the question, whether Virginia or Massachusetts struck the first and decisive blow. The debate, in feigned mutual difference, and sweet complacency, always proceeded on the thought, that those two most important and meritorious states, solely begun, sustained and accomplished the revolution. That all the other states, had hardly an interest or a participation. Rhode Island and the Gaspee it was always convenient to forget. It is from foreign, and impartial historians, that we are reminded of the relative importance of that deed, which first impressed a bloody hue on our proceeding, and doomed its perpetrators, if the virtue of the country could have permitted their detection, to irremissible death.

As to the effect produced by this daring act, and its baffled prosecution, the dread of ministerial vengeance, and the deep but calm determination to meet that vengeance, I must depend on tradition, and appeal to the recollections of the few survivors, of that portentous period. The effect was universal. The flames of the Gaspee seem to have been not only seen, but felt throughout the continent.

Independence, unqualified independence, was the aim of Rhode-Island, and it proceeded accordingly. In 1774 you did an act, if possible, more positive, daring, and decisive, more unequivocally indicative of your warlike spirit and your determination to be independent. You rose, as the British lawyers said, from common felony to high and atrocious treason. As soon as the proclamation, prohibiting the importation of arms from England, was known here, you dismantled the king's fort at Newport, and took possession of 40 pieces of cannon. All our leading men, not only had at heart, but avowed the same sentiment as that contained in General Greene's letter to Governor Ward, then a member of the first Congress, dated on the 4th of June, 1774, at the camp on Prospect hill. "Permit me," says he then, "to recommend from the sincerity of my heart, ready at all times to bleed in my country's cause, a declaration of independence, and call upon the world and the great God who governs it, to witness the propriety and rectitude thereof." We anticipated Congress in the declaration of independence ; for, by a solemn act of our General Assembly, we dissolved all connexion with Great Britain, in the May previous. We withdrew our allegiance from the king, and renounced his government forever, and, in a declaration of independence we put down in a condensed, logical statement, our unanswerable reasons for so doing. I drew my facts from records, nothing is colored or exaggerated.

Our conduct in the war, was in perfect keeping with our previous character. The news of the battle of Lexington, reached this town on the evening of the same day, the 19th of April, 1776. In spite of the evasions and vacillations of the Governor and Lieutenant-Governor, three days after you poured your hasty levies of militia, a large detachment, into Massachusetts. In the same year you raised and had in service 1200 regular troops. You afterwards raised three state regiments, and this from a population of about 50,000 souls—an astonishing fact! According to Gibbon, the calculation confirmed by the experience of all ages, is that a community that sends into the field more than the one hundredth part of its population, will soon perish from exhaustion. You did vastly more than this—voluntarily more than Bonaparte in his severest conscription ever dared demand. The truth is, your spirit was high and warm, your generosity reckless, your soaring, romantic. It is one of the few evils amidst the innumerable blessings of a confederacy, composed of states of unequal territory and population that the small must from the nature of things, contribute more in proportion than the larger state; it can be more easily congregated and excited. The flashes of sentiment are conducted from one to another, and to the whole with electric celerity. The citizens are prompt in the performance of what they promptly resolve. They bear the burden, they fight the battle, they shout the victory, and returning from its well fought field, descry the tardy contingents of larger and perhaps wiser states, plodding their cautious way to see, to admire and perchance to envy, what has been done.

You took high ground by your members in Congress, as to the mode of conducting the war. You endeavored to give it a naval cast. Distinguished for your commercial marine, and for the enterprize and intrepidity of your mariners, you felt the necessity and urged the expediency of naval military exertion. The first little fleet, the germ, the nautilus of our present naval character and fame, was commanded by a native Rhode-Islander, Commodore Esek Hopkins, who surprised New Providence, captured the governor, lieutenant governor and other officers of the crown, seized a hundred pieces of cannon, and carried off all the munitions of war from the island. The island was occupied for weeks, and with what is and I hope ever will be the characteristic of American and Rhode-Island commanders, with a most scrupulous respect for private property and individual feeling.

My humble attempt, hitherto, has been that of suggesting the general national spirit that led to, and effected, our revolution, and the particular, but efficient share that, from institution, character and pre-disposition, Rhode-Island contributed to the main design. This last attempt, will be blamed, as fostering a delusive vanity, and deceptive self-esteem. But if individuals have a natural right to feel a generous consciousness of a pure and virtuous ancestry—if the Romans placed in the vestibules of their houses, the statues of their progenitors, that they might, by beholding them as they passed, be excited to a rivalry of their excellence, surely you as a state, have a peculiar and indubitable right, to indulge in a state pride. It is justified from the purified and pious motives which impelled to your primary institution, as a body politic, and which conducted, continued, and upheld you in the same direction, through all your difficulties, dangers, and distresses, through good report and evil report, even unto the end. That, which in the individual is a selfish or absurd vanity, diffused, mitigated, and generalized by a community, is patriotism—the cement of union—the spring of virtuous emulation—the nurse of lofty thoughts, and the impulse of heroic deeds. Rhode-Island has had as yet no historian; of our heroes and sages it may indeed be said—"they had no poet, and they died."

THE BATTLE OF BENNINGTON

BY THOMAS P. RODMAN.

Up through a cloudy sky, the sun
 Was buffeting his way,
On such a morn as ushers in
 A sultry August day.
Hot was the air—and hotter yet
 Men's thoughts within them grew:
They Britons, Hessians, Tories saw—
 They saw their homesteads too.

They thought of all their country's wrongs,
 They thought of noble lives
Poured out in battle with her foes,
 They thought upon their wives,
Their children and their aged sires,
 Their firesides, churches, God—
And these deep thoughts made hallowed ground
 Each foot of soil they trod.

Their leader was a brave old man,
 A man of earnest will;
His very presence was a host—
 He'd fought at Bunker Hill.
A living monument he stood
 Of stirring deeds of fame,

Of deeds that shed a fadeless light
  On his own deathless name.

Of Charlestown's flames, of Warren's blood,
  His presence told the tale,
It made each hero's heart beat high
  Though lip and cheek grew pale ;
It spoke of Princetown, Morristown,
  Told Trenton's thrilling story—
It lit futurity with hope,
  And on the past shed glory.

Who were those men, their leader who?
  Where stood they on that morn?
The men were Berkshire yeomanry,
  Brave men as e'er were born,—
Who in the reaper's merry row
  Or warrior rank could stand ;
Right worthy such a noble troop,
  John Stark led on the band.

Wollamsac wanders by the spot
  Where they that morning stood;
Then rolled the war cloud o'er the stream,
  The waves were tinged with blood ;
And the near hills that dark cloud girt
  And fires like lightning flashed,
And shrieks and groans like howling blasts
  Rose as the bayonets clashed.

The night before, the Yankee host
  Came gathering from afar,
And in each belted bosom glowed
  The spirit of the war.
All full of fight through rainy storm,
  Night, cloudy, starless, dark
They came, and gathered as they came,
  Around the valiant Stark.

There was a Berkshire parson—he
  And all his flock were there,
And like true churchmen militant
  The arm of flesh made bare.
Out spake the Dominie and said,
  "For battle have we come
These many times, and after this
  We mean to stay at home."

If now we come in vain, said Stark,
  What! will you go to-night
To battle it with yonder troops,
  God send us morning light,
And we will give you work enough:
  Let but the morning come,
And if ye hear no voice of war,
  Go back and stay at home.

The morning came—there stood the foe,
  Stark eyed them as they stood—

Few words he spake—'t was not a time
For moralising mood.
"See there the enemy, my boys!
Now strong in valor's might,
Beat them, or Molly Stark will sleep
In widowhood to-night."

Each soldier there had left at home
A sweetheart, wife, or mother,
A blooming sister, or, perchance,
A fair-haired, blue-eyed brother.
Each from a fireside came, and thoughts
Those simple words awoke
That nerved up every warrior's arm
And guided every stroke.

Fireside and woman—mighty words!
How wondrous is the spell
They work upon the manly heart,
Who knoweth not full well?
And, than the women of this land,
That never land hath known
A truer, prouder hearted race,
Each Yankee boy must own.

Brief eloquence was Stark's—nor vain—
Scarce uttered he the words,
When burst the musket's rattling peal
Out leaped the flashing swords;

And when brave Stark in after time
  Told the proud tale of wonder
He said the battle din was one
  " Continual clap of thunder."

Two hours they strove—then victory crowned
  The gallant Yankee boys.
Nought but the memory of the dead
  Bedimmed their glorious joys ;
Aye—there's the rub—the hour of strife,
  Though follow years of fame,
Is still in mournful memory linked
  With some death-hallowed name.

The cypress with the laurel twines—
  The pæan sounds a knell,
The trophied column marks the spot
  Where friends and brothers fell.
Fame's mantle a funereal pall
  Seems to the grief dimmed eye,
For ever where the bravest fall
  The best beloved die.

THE EFFECTS OF SIN.

BY REV. FRANCIS VINTON.

WHEN man came forth from the hands of God, he was upright, holy, perfect ; and God pronounced him *very good.*

Not one stain of sin tarnished his moral nature. He was the image of God. Not a pang, nor a sorrow troubled his soul. He was the mirror of the divine happiness because he reflected the divine holiness. In original humanity what harmony, what beauty dwelt! It was a harp of many strings ; but all were tuned by the Maker, and were struck into music by a heaven taught hand. It was a glorious humanity. Each faculty indeed was distinct like the colors of the rainbow, but they all were combined and melted into one another, shining forth as the brightness of the Father's glory—and as man trod the ground, the earth beheld the likeness of God.

Man sinned—the harp was broken—the strings were untuned, and instead of harmony, was discord. *He sinned*—the mirror was in fragments, each was stained, and soiled, and now reflected the distorted image of the Maker.

Man sinned. And the beauty of those blended colors was destroyed. Instead of the mild, and genial radiance of sunshine, was the glaring of fire. Hot passions burned furiously in that heart where pure affections had shone gently, and this altar of heaven became a laboratory of hell.—*Man sinned.* The fresh, and laughing earth now groaned. The thorn, and thistle now sprang forth. The eye of the lion, and the tiger now shot glances of enmity, and savage lust, ravenous desires, and cruelty now circulated throughout the animate creation.

Man sinned, and all was *cursed.* Death made havoc first in Paradise, and sent decay, and sickness over every created thing. The exquisite body of man, which had stood like a finished temple, monumental of the skill of its architect, crumbled. Next to the soul, it was death's chiefest prey, and under his touch it was dissolved into dust. In the strong language of Scripture "Death *reigned.*" He was Lord paramount over earth, and swayed his sceptre as king of terrors. By one man sin entered into the world, and death by sin, and so death passed upon all men. He was indeed an enemy. Had sin spoiled man alone, its ravages had been less fearful ; but every creature was made subject to vanity, and delivered over to the bondage of corruption, and so the whole creation groaneth and travaileth together in pain until now. All evil, and all death, are the fruits of the sin of Adam. The curse was upon all things, and annihilation brooded on every creature that God had made.

ODE TO THE POPPY.

BY CYNTHIA TAGGART.*

THOUGH varied wreaths of myriad hues,
  As beams of mingling light,
Sparkle replete with pearly dews,
Waving their tinted leaves profuse,
  To captivate the sight:

Though fragrance, sweet exhaling, blend
  With the soft, balmy air;
And gentle zephyrs, wafting wide,
  Their spicy odors bear;
      While to the eye,
      Delightingly,
  Each floweret laughing blooms,
      And o'er the fields
      Prolific, yields
  Its incense of perfumes;

*Note 3.—See Appendix.

Yet one alone o'er all the plain,
With lingering eye I view ;
Hasty, I pass the brightest bower,
Heedless of each attractive power,
Its brilliance to pursue.

No odors sweet proclaim the spot,
Where its soft leaves unfold ;
Nor mingled hues of beauty bright
Charm and allure the captive sight,
With forms and tints untold.

One simple hue the plant portrays
Of glowing radiance rare,
Fresh as the roseate morn displays,
And seeming sweet and fair.

But closer prest, an odorous breath
Repels the rover gay ;
And from her hand with eager haste
'T is careless thrown away ;

And thoughtless, that in evil hour
Disease may happiness devour,
And her fair form, elastic now,
To misery's wand may hopeless bow.

Then Reason leads sad Sorrow forth,
To seek this lonely flower ;

And blest experience kindly proves
  Its mitigating power.

Then, its bright hue the sight can trace,
  The brilliance of its bloom;
Though misery veil the weeping eyes,
Though sorrow choke the breath with sighs,
  And life deplore its doom.

    This magic flower
    In desperate hour,
  A balsam mild shall yield,
    When the sad, sinking heart
    Feels every aid depart,
  And every gate of hope forever sealed.

    Then shall its potent charm
    Each agony disarm,
  And its all-healing power shall respite give.
    The frantic sufferer, then,
    Convulsed and wild with pain,
  Shall own the sovereign remedy, and live.

    The dews of slumber, now,
    Rest on her aching brow;
  And o'er the languid lids, balsamic fall;
    While fainting nature hears,
    With dissipated fears,
  The lowly accents of soft Somnus' call.

Then will affection twine
  Around this kindly flower ;
And grateful memory keep,
How, in the arms of sleep,
  Affliction lost its power.

THOUGHTS ON EDUCATION.

BY ZACHARIAH ALLEN.

HOWEVER varied are the occupations of men, one pursuit is common to all, that of happiness. The principal obstacle to success in this pursuit, is ignorance ;—ignorance of the rational mode of obtaining it.

Plato often repeated to his disciples, "that all vice springs from ignorance ;" and that it is a want of proper instruction alone, that can lead a man into the great mistake of following a vicious course, because it seems to lead directly to some good, greater than any which a virtuous course may promise. A practical statesman of the present age, the King of Prussia, in accordance with the doctrine of Plato, considers that no parent has a right to inflict so great an injury on society, as to bring up his child in ignorance ; and has enforced by compulsory laws on all parents in his dominions, the duty of attending to the cultivation of the minds of their children.

Euclid maintained, that knowledge only is required to direct every man in the path most conducive to his happiness, and boldly asserted the startling doctrine, deduced from this proposition, that "there is actually no necessary evil." In illustration of this doctrine, one of the most popular philosophers of our own time, Mr. Combe, observes, that under the benign influence of Christianity and revelation, the most delightful view in which the goodness and beneficence of the Almighty can be placed before us, is, that the constitution of our natures, and the moral laws by which the world is governed, are such as lead always to good when their dictates are obeyed: whereas the least infringement of them is attended by some warning, erroneously called evil. Education will teach us that all which we call evil, is in reality most benevolently designated for *good*, as it is a warning for our instruction, to return to, or adopt the proper course;—the course prescribed by those laws; that, in fact, "evil does not, cannot exist."

When the improvement of the mind, the source and seat of enjoyment is left neglected, it is not a matter of surprise that dissatisfaction should be experienced by those, who with undue zeal devote their time and exertions to gaining wealth or fame, or to the indulgence of sensual pleasures. Even Solomon required the practical lessons of experience to discover, that the engrossing pursuit of them, is nothing but "vanity and vexation of spirit."

In the liberal professions, should unintermitted cares of business exclusively absorb attention, the scholar may become inferior in mental cultivation to many mechanics ; and although situated on the brink of the fountain of science, he may then devote himself rather to stooping down in search of gold among the sands, than to tasting of the inspiring waters.

To the young man, entering on the active scenes of life, with generous feelings of ambition to excel, a taste for the acquisition of knowledge renders him cheerful and happy, and proves a safeguard to preserve him from temptations to evil. Refined mental enjoyments, and gross, debasing pleasures are seldom relished by the same individual. The one or the other will speedily assume the control over the mind, which rarely acknowledges a divided empire. It is like Mohammedan fatalism voluntarily to remain in ignorance of the knowledge that may deliver us from evil ; or like the rashness of the mariner, who launches his bark to navigate the wide ocean, and neglects to make use of the discoveries of science to direct his course and to preserve him from the perils of the deep.

Theatrical exhibitions would comparatively lose their demoralizing attractions, were magnificent theatres erected for the interesting display of splendid philosophical lectures and experiments, and were men of science and eloquence recompensated with a liberality equal to that bestowed upon Opera dancers. It is only necessary to lend the aid of the charms of music and painting, in brilliantly illuminated halls, to those of eloquent public lecturers, to produce excitement on the minds of the young, and to ensure the decision of the public taste in their favor. Properly qualified, eloquent lecturers, are now wanting to minister to this improved public taste ; and no professional occupation would be more productive of certain and munificent emolument.

The political axiom of our republican code of government, affirming that all men are born equal, goes no further than to place men on the same footing or standing in the great race of human competition. Education, partially diffused, has the immediate effect to produce inequality ; for mental powers unimproved are of as little avail as the churl's politeness, who said that he was born with as much as Chesterfield himself, and was confident that he had never diminished his stock by use.

It is not by classing the learned, the good and the great men of our land on a level with the indolent and vicious, that men are to be brought to a happy state of equality ; but on the contrary by exalting the poor and the depressed by means of the diffusion of knowledge. General and thorough education is the true *levelling principle.* By the aid of very limited means of self instruction, persons commencing life as humble day laborers, have risen and will continue to rise, to the first distinctions of honor in our country. Although it is certain that mechanics do not often become philosophers, yet it is equally certain that they have, by means of self instruction become the greatest of philosophers. With laudable inducements to tempt him forward in his inventions, the mechanic feels in a degree the ardor which inspires the philosopher or the soldier, to leave a name that will survive in the recollection of successive generations, as long as the grass continue to cover with fresh verdure, the earth above his grave. After thousands of years shall have rolled away, and the very monuments of philosophers, statesmen and warriors of renown shall have been crumbled to dust, the multitude of human beings who may then people this earth, will as frequently recur to the popular name of him, whose genius first introduced the use of the steamboat and enabled man to overpower the swift currents of adverse tides, as to the memory of Newton who explained the great laws that govern those tides.

Although a young man may fail in his attempts to amass wealth, to enable him to make a distinguished appearance in the gay circles of fashion, yet it is in his power to qualify himself by mental cultivation, to associate with a superior class of men, who value the aristocracy of mind, above that of wealth. He may thus attain a more truly respectable standing, and enjoy more rational pleasures, than the absorbing pursuit of wealth can afford. On every side he will find objects to interest and delight. Should he engage in the study of animal life, a vast range for research is presented him, in the thousands of species of animals and of the insect tribes. Of animalculæ, the numbers are beyond the power of computation, and their minuteness is still more wonderful ; as a few cubic feet of sea water gives full scope for all the enjoyments of vitality to more of them, than there are human inhabitants on the earth. Yet all these minute beings exhibit to the eye of the scientific observer, by the aid of glasses, perfectly organized structures like those of large animals, having arteries, nerves and circulating blood. If he turn his attention to Botany he will find that seventy or eighty thousand distinct species of plants decorate the surface of the earth with their bright colors, or vegetate in the dark caves of the ocean.

Days may be passed in admiring the varied forms and glowing tints of the different classes of shells. Mountains are formed of the limestone, products of shell-fish, and countless islands of the sea have been created by the coral reefs, constructed by a feeble worm. The earliest history of the earth itself the student will find recorded in the impressions, on buried rocks, from whence the petrified remains of numerous, and now extinct species of animal and vegetables are constantly brought to light.

In addition to all these are the numerous subjects contained in the long catalogue of useful knowledge, which are adapted to improve and elevate the mind. But if he flag in his ardor for investigating terrestrial objects, he has only to lift his eyes to the glorious firmament of Heaven. His imagination in the boldness of its flight, may visit unseen worlds, numerous as particles of floating dust, until wearied in its boundless course, it may at last rest in silent awe before the throne of Him who created them.

Oh! cold indeed must be the feelings of that man who can contemplate all these objects without emotion. But the ordinary term of human life would neither be sufficient to learn nor to relate in detail, all the interesting works of creation. Were we able to attempt a narration of them, the decrepitude of age might steal over us, and still our task would be but commenced. The dull, cold ear of death would at last remain insensible to the voice that might be addressed to it, in continued utterance of the exhaustless descriptions. But the pleasing hope may animate us, that gathered from time to eternity and joining with the worshipping host of Heaven, it may constitute a part of our happiness, as all seeing, celestial spirits, to rejoice in beholding clearly and comprehensibly, and not as now "through a glass darkly," with the feeble vision of montal eyes, the interminable display of the wondrous works of our great Creator.

PETTIQUAMSCOTT.*

BY EMMA ROBINSON.

WHAT e'er can warm the imagination,
Please the eye, or charm the ear ;
In enchanting variation,
Bounteous nature lavished here.

Pious awe and sweet composure
This sequestered gloom inspires,
And from this secure enclosure
Every ruder thought retires.

Here the waters idly sporting,
Fondly woo the grassy shore ;
And more calm recesses courting,
Shun the ocean's stormy war.

Here, more tranquil joys pursuing,
Pettiquamscott steals away ;
Oft his peaceful course reviewing,
Winds along with sweet delay.

Moss-grown rocks their heads erecting,
Heighten still the pleasing gloom ;
And their circling flowers protecting,
Bid them unmolested bloom.

* Near Point Judith.

Here the birds the sunbeams flying,
Nature's inspiration sing ;
Echo to their voice replying,
Makes the neighboring valleys ring.

This fair spot with partial pleasure,
Pettiquamscott's arms entwine ;
Leaves with pain his favorite treasure,
Parting feels regret like mine.

Soon again thy waves returning,
Shall embrace this peaceful shore ;
Fate my fondest wishes spurning
Bids me different scenes explore.

Follow still thy sweet employment
Wave ye woods, ye oceans roar ;
You shall give sublime enjoyment,
When your Emma is no more.

1785.

THE CULTIVATION OF TASTE.

BY THE REV. WILLIAM HAGUE.

The importance of cultivating a correct taste for natural and moral beauty has often been inculcated by the novelist and philosopher, the preacher and the poet. Its effects prove its worth. It expands the mind and refines the heart, it alleviates the ills of life, and multiplies its joys, it soothes the agitations of the troubled bosom and throws a genial sunlight around the calm and placid spirit; it constantly opens new and pleasing paths of pursuit, leads to new springs of happiness, and diffuses its own fresh charm around the whole creation. He who has cultivated as he may, his natural susceptibility of deriving delight from the beautiful in nature or the sublime in morals, the lights of science or the charms of art, has within himself a source of high enjoyment, which delivers him from the thraldom of gross appetite, the corrosion of petty cares, and the many irritations which arise amid the hurry and tumult of life. The more delicate his taste becomes, the more nice is he in his discrimination of character, the more keenly alive to the pleasures of friendship, the more susceptible of the soft and tender emotions, the more delighted with tranquil scenes, the more disposed to calm reflection. He has a zest for joys of which others do not dream, and even the character of his sorrows is peculiar, for they are changed into an agreeable melancholy which soothes the heart that feels its weight, and has a natural affinity for all that is exalted in genius, or tender in sympathy, or commanding in moral greatness, or glowing in fancy. Such an one, though familiar with the world in which the worldling lives, yet lives himself in a world which we may call his own. He sees glories around him to which others are blind. He hears a music, which others do not hear. He feels a rapture which is real, but which he can not communicate, and in which only kindred minds can sympathize. Not that the elements of his nature differ from those others, only they are differently developed. The boor who gazes at night upon the vaulted firmament, sees nothing there but "twinkling lamps to light him home." The man of cultivated taste sees worlds on worlds, an "infinite amaze," a scene of wondrous order and magnificence, proclaiming the Creator's presence and making known that he is Love ; the moon walking in her brightness,

> And nightly to the listening earth
> Repeats the story of her birth,
> While all the stars around her burn,
> And all the planets in their turn
> Confirm the tidings as they roll
> And spread the truth from pole to pole.

But while the importance of cultivating good taste may be conceded in general terms, the question may arise, what is good taste ? Is there any thing fixed in its character ? Are there any established principles by which it is governed ? Is there any room for appeal beyond a man's own feelings respecting what is truly beautiful? Has it not long since passed into a popular maxim "*de gustibus non disputandum;*" and is it not bringing a question at once to an issue, to say of the subject of it, "it is a mere matter of taste?" In regard to what is true and what is false, we may appeal from opinions to facts. We may show what has real existence. But in regard to what is beautiful and what is deformed, can we appeal to any thing beyond the sentiment of the mind? It is the mind which throws out its own inward light over various objects and thence views them as beautiful.

> Mind, mind alone (bear witness earth and Heaven)
> The living fountains in itself contains
> Of beauteous and sublime; here hand in hand
> Sit paramount the Graces.

Thence if I *feel* any thing to be beautiful, is it not therefore, truly beautiful, and even more beauteous still, because I cannot see why it is so?

Undoubtedly it is true that there is in no object an inherent beauty any more than there is inherent color; that it is the mind which conceives the idea of beauty and connects it with the external object—the mind which, by its sensibility and its power of association invests the universe with its loveliness.

But then, has not the inward world its *laws* as well as the outward? Is not the one adjusted to the other? Is there not a harmony in their operations? May not the moral sense and the sense of beauty be as uniform and determinate as the animal senses, though modified like every part of human nature, by circumstances? What if a man should declare that the monotonous tones of a public crier are as musical and beautiful as the varied intonations of the orator on whose lips senates hang enraptured? Or, that the notes which reach his ear from the hand-organ borne by the music-grinder through the street, are as beautiful and elevating as those which break from the mighty instrument of Harlem, when, under the touch of a master's hand, it pours its bounding notes along? Or, what if one should see as much beauty in the paltry decorations of an eastern Pagoda as in the simple front of the Pantheon, or the majestic dome of St. Peter's? Or, what if one should be delighted to place amidst a group of pendant willows in a cemetery the tall and straight limbed poplar, which presents not a mere contrast, but a direct opposition of features? In such cases our sensibility to beauty is somewhat shocked; all feel that some law of nature is violated, and look on him who so confounds things that differ, or delights in aught so incongruous, as void of all taste. Hence we learn that there are established principles of taste, that the laws of this part of our constitution are as fixed as those of any other ; and that within its sphere, order reigns as wisely and supremely as in that part of speculative opinion. Yea, far more so. In the world of philosophy, Greece has long since ceased to rule, but in the realm of taste she is still the "star ascendant." Her theories of nature have passed away like brilliant dreams, but her works of taste still live to captivate the world. Her architecture still stands in all the dignity of its fair proportions, her statues still speak, her poetry still glows with living fire, her oratory still wakes a genial enthusiasm, as when it roused in the dormant multitude a voice like the voice of many waters and the voice of mighty thunderings, crying "let us march against Philip, let us conquer or die." The speculations of Cicero have withered under the touch of time, but the eloquence which first stirred Roman blood, still quickens the pulsations of an American assembly. Longinus, who, centuries ago, swayed a mighty sceptre as the prince of critics, still stands invested with unfading honors. The theology of Milton has made but a slight impression on mankind, but his poetry will

20

warm the hearts and stimulate the intellects of far distant generations. The same Homer, who was once the delight of Greece, still pleases us; the same Virgil, who was the boast and ornament of Rome, now receives every where the homage due to genius. The productions of mind which evince only great intellectual power, or depth of thought, or wide research, may yet be doomed to perish and be forgotten; but true beauty lives forever and wins a universal sway.

Still, if beauty be not a mere airy fiction but a substantial reality, the question yet arises, how may we define that taste for beauty which may be justly designated as good and correct? Objects which are regarded as beautiful in one age, are utterly neglected in another, and loathed in a third. During the prevalence of any particular fashion, it is deemed a proof of bad taste to decry it, and if one should attempt it, on what grounds could he justify himself? He might say of any ornament, or dress, or piece of music, "it offends me;" to which another might reply, "it pleases me;" and so the argument is at an end. What then is the criterion of good taste?

Here, it is worthy of remark, that there is an analogy between that faculty of the soul which we denominate *Taste*, and that Physical faculty which we call by the same name. The latter is given to us, not merely as a means of pleasure, but also in in order to distinguish between those substances which are good for food and those which are noxious. In a healthy state it answers this end. If, however, you observe an individual whose taste constantly craves varieties and stimulants, loathing those simple articles of refreshment which nature has so richly provided for us, you say at once, his taste is perverted—it is at variance with the laws of his nature. There you strike a far-reaching principle. If a man seek as food what exhausts rather than nourishes his frame, if he is fascinated with what is ruinous, you say his taste is not in accordance with natural laws, and thence it is bad. The rule is universal. Good taste, either within the sphere of the material world, or the spiritual world, is that which is in harmony with the laws of the universe. The more you know of these, the more numerous criteria will you have to ascertain whether your taste be healthy or disordered. The more you study these with such views, the more conformed will your taste become, to that of the infinite and eternal mind, whose ideas of beauty are bodied forth in this vast creation, which, as at his bidding, it sprang from chaos into order, reflecting in all its heights and depths the beauteous and sublime conceptions of its author, he looked upon with delight, and pronounced it *good.*

The power of perceiving beauty, of being fascinated with it, of receiving deeper and deeper impression from it, distinguishes a rational mind. and forms a part of that stamp of natural dignity, which was originally placed upon the brow of man. He was formed to look upon the material universe as a glorious mirror, reflecting every where goodness, grandeur, beauty, sublimity.

What then is taste, but these internal powers,
Active and strong, and feelingly alive
To each fine impulse? A discovering sense
Of decent and sublime, with quick disgust
From things deformed, or disarranged, or gross
In species? This, nor gems, nor stores of gold,
Nor purple state, nor culture can bestow,
But God alone, when first his active hand
Imprints the secret bias of the soul.

The mighty Parent, wise and just in all,
Free as the vital breeze or light of Heaven
Reveals the charms of Nature. Ask the swain
Who journeys homeward from a summer day's
Long labor, why forgetful of his toils,
And due repose he loiters to behold
The sunshine gleaming as thro' amber clouds
O'er all the western sky. Full soon I ween,
His rude expression and untutored airs,
Beyond the power of language will unfold
The form of beauty smiling at his heart,
How lovely! How commanding!

But although it be true that culture can never bestow the faculty of taste upon man, yet without culture the germ can never be developed. Now what are the means of cultivating it? In answering this question,—

Our *first* observation is, that if good taste be that which is in harmony with the laws of the universe, then the most important means of cultivating it, is *to become acquainted with those laws*. He who made the human mind, made all worlds, and a glorious harmony pervades them. He hath garnished the heavens, adorned the world with loveliness, and inspired the mind with a taste for beauty. The great fabric of creation through which order reigns, is the development of that love for natural and moral beauty, which dwelt from eternity in the Infinite mind. Our emotions of beauty, therefore, are modified by an acquaintance with those laws which shine out in the operations of nature, either within the spiritual or the material realm. We are so constituted as to see a moral beauty in benevolence, and the more clearly we discern the law by which it is connected with peace of mind and social happiness, the more beauty shall we see in it and love it more. We are so formed as to admire the heroism which is enjoyed in sacrificing the pleasures of sense, or stores of gold to the interests of virtue ; and the more clearly we see the law, that man was created to obey his moral sentiments, which hold by right the throne of the soul, the more enamored shall we be with the beauty of virtue.

This enlargement of mind of which we speak, produced by an extensive acquaintance with the laws of nature, physical or moral, with the established principles of art and science, will evidently affect our emotions of taste, by inducing new associations of ideas, and new trains of feeling. To a man entirely ignorant of the laws of life, the slender compressed and tapering waist of a human form may seem beautiful, as the expression of delicacy, symmetry and refinement ; but let him conceive aright of the tender vital organs unnaturally cramped and denied the free and easy play so essential to life and health, then the spell would at once be broken, and pain succeed to pleasure. As the serpentine motion expressive of delicacy and ease, delights us in every case except that of the serpent itself, where the thought of malignity and peril is awakened, so here, the pleasure of discovering an extraordinary symmetry and delicacy of the human form is dispelled by the ideas of constraint, and pain, and danger, which a compression of that form tends always to produce.

"Nothing is beautiful but what is true," say the Rhetoricians. This is a universal maxim. Conformity to truth is beauty, real and permanent. Study nature. Seek truth. The laws of nature are distinguished by simplicity, and simplicity has an abiding charm whether it appear in literature or art, in character or manners. Thence affectation always displeases when it is discovered. Though affectation be the fashion, yet it appears contemptible as soon as it loses the delusive charm of novelty or a name. In France, fashion once declared for an affected negligence of dress. Thence we hear Montaigne saying, "I have never yet been apt to imitate the negligent garb, observable among the young men of our time, to wear my cloak on one shoulder, my bonnet on one side, and one stocking in somewhat more disorder than the other, meant to express a manly disdain of such exotic ornaments, and a contempt of art." There is no beauty in the *cultivated* negligence even of trifles. It is only that which is occasional, appropriate, and which indicates a mind engaged and absorbed in something worthy of it which truly pleases. Scott saw it in his Lady of the Lake, when he said,

"With head upraised, and look intent,
And eye and ear attentive bent,
And locks flung back, and lips apart,
Like monument of Grecian art,
In listening mood she seemed to stand,
The guardian Naiad of the strand."

No kindred grace adorns her of whom it may be said

Coquet and coy, at once her air,
Both studied, tho' both seem neglected ;
Careless she is with artful care
Affecting to seem unaffected.

Truth to nature, then, is beauty, and to study the laws of nature is to chasten and develope the taste for beauty.

Another means of cultivating good taste, is to study the *expression of character or design* in which the beauty of objects consists. In the material world, every thing beautiful, is a manifestion of certain qualities which are by nature agreeable to the mind ; and to ascertain what these are, to point them out distinctly, to classify them, is a pleasing mode of refining and quickening the taste for beauty. "The longer I live," said one, "the more familiar I become with the world around me. Oh! that I could feel the keen zest of which I was susceptible when a boy, and all was new and fair!" "The longer I live," says another, "the more charmed I become with the beauties of a picture or a landscape." The first of these had a natural taste for beauty which he had never developed by studying the expressions of character, which constitute the loveliness of creation. The other, regarding the outward universe as a splendid system of signs directed his attention to the thing signified ; loved to contemplate the moral qualities which were beaming forth from all the surrounding objects, and thus saw open before him a boundless field, ever glowing with new colors and fresh attractions. The first, as he heard a piece of music, might from the mechanism of his nature feel some pleasure arising from novelty, or a regular succession of sounds, which familiarity would soon dispel. The other, as he studied the expression of character, which those tones gave forth, as for instance, with the loud sound he associated the ideas of power or peril, with the low, those of delicacy and gentleness, with the acute, those of fear or surprise, with the grave, solemnity and dignity ; he would become more and more deeply touched and enraptured, while listening to the music of nature in the voice of singing winds or in the plaint of an Æolian harp, in the crash of thunder or in the roar of the Cataract, in the murmur of the brook or in the moan of the ocean, in the sigh of the zephyr or in the breath of the whirlwind, or while listening to the music of art breaking forth from the loud-sounding trumpet, the muffled drum, or Zion's lyre which hangs upon religion's shrine.

CHARLIE MACHREE.

A BALLAD.

BY WILLIAM J. HOPPIN.

I.

Come over, come over
 The river to me,
If ye are my laddie,
 Bold Charlie Machree.

Here's Mary McPherson,
 And Susey O'Linn,
Who say ye're faint-hearted,
 And darena plunge in.

But the dark rolling water
 Though deep as the sea,
I know willna scare ye,
 Nor keep ye frae me:

For stout is ye'r back,
 And strong is ye'r arm,
And the heart in ye'r bosom
 Is faithful and warm.

Come over, come over
  The river to me,
If ye are my laddie
  Bold Charlie Machree!

II.

I see him, I see him,
  He 's plunged in the tide,
His strong arms are dashing
  The big waves aside;

Oh, the dark rolling water
  Shoots swift as the sea,
But blythe is the glance
  Of his bonny blue e'e;

And his cheeks are like roses,
  Twa buds on a bough;
Who says ye 're faint-hearted
  My brave Charlie now?

Ho, ho, foaming river,
  Ye may roar as ye go,
But ye canna bear Charlie
  To the dark loch below!

Come over, come over
  The river to me,
My true hearted laddie,
  My Charlie Machree!

III.

He's sinking, he's sinking,
  Oh, what shall I do!
Strike out, Charlie, boldly,
  Ten strokes and ye're thro'.

He's sinking, oh Heaven!
  Ne'er fear, man, ne'er fear,
I've a kiss for ye, Charlie,
  As soon as ye're here!

He rises, I see him,
  Five strokes, Charlie, mair—
He 's shaking the wet
  From his bonny brown hair.

He conquers the current,
  He gains on the sea,
Ho, where is the swimmer
  Like Charlie Machree!

Come over the river,
  But *once* come to me,
And I 'll love ye forever
  Dear Charlie Machree.

IV.

He 's sinking, he 's gone,
  Oh God, it is I,
It is I who have killed him,
  Help, help—he must die!

Help, help—ah, he rises—
  Strike out and ye're free,
Ho, bravely done, Charlie,
  Once more now, for me!

Now cling to the rock—
  Now gie us ye'r hand—
Ye 're safe, dearest Charlie,
  Ye 're safe on the land!

Come lie in my bosom,
  If *there* ye can sleep,
I canna speak to ye,
  I only can weep.

Ye 've crossed the wild river,
  Ye 've risked all for me,
And I 'll part frae ye never
  Dear Charlie Machree!

OLD AGE.

BY THE REV. EDWARD B. HALL.

LIFE presents few images of higher beauty, than that of a tranquil and virtuous old age. It is quite distinct from the beauty and power of all other periods. The innocence of infancy has a charm unsurpassed in its kind, nor are they to be envied who cannot see it. The simplicity of childhood finds its way to every heart, which selfishness has not cased, or system perverted. The buoyancy of youth, especially when subdued by the gentle hand of religion and gladdened by her smile, is inexpressibly lovely. And the sober strength of manhood, putting itself forth for the good of society and the enduring interests of man, is an object on which the eyes of all, even of the frivolous and corrupt, love to rest, or are forced to look with respect. But you will pass them all, if you see beyond them the venerable form, erect in its dignity, or bending with its load of years well-filled. Here is maturity. And if it has been attained beneath the warmth and is tinged with the rays of the sun of righteousness, there is a grandeur in its beauty, a majesty in its calmness, a mellowness and richness in its fruits, to which none can be indifferent. Even when it is broken with the infirmities of old age, when the senses are dulled, the mind impaired, and the multitude of years has become labor and sorrow, it is an object of deep respect and unusual interest, to every mind that respects itself and every heart that is interested in its race. For, beside the intrinsic venerableness of age, varied but never destroyed by circumstances, there will come occasional words of far-reaching recollection, brief hints full of experience and instruction, voices of warning, breaking upon the ear like the voices of the dead, and at times flashes of light issuing from hidden depths—all telling of an age that is past, and a soul that cannot decay. Then, as the shades of death creep on, see the tranquillity with which its approach is often watched, the subdued joy with which it is welcomed, the kind but unsparing faithfulness with which it is improved for the instruction of those around. And when (as we sometimes see in the saddest yet noblest wrecks, and to us among the valued tokens of the souls immortality) the worn out frame loses at last even its power of burdening and clouding, and the spirit which for a time had been its prisoner becomes again its Monarch, emerging from its dungeon darkness and reascending its throne of light, how unearthly does it appear,—how resistlessly does it command the perishing organs, its sensual servants, to do its will, or act as if now independent of their ministry! The sunken frame lifts itself up with a strength not its own, the drooping arm is new-nerved, the listless eye beams with no common light, the faltering voice recovers and deepens fearfully its tone, and the shrivelled lips, touched with an eloquence as of another world, give forth in moments volumes of gathered wisdom. It is not the master of fiction alone who has drawn a picture of such majesty in age and renovation in decay, nor imagination only that has dipped its pencil in these colors. It is reality. It is the Master of nature and man, the Framer of these bodies and Father of these spirits. It is He who hath said, " Even to your old age, I am He ; and even to hoary hairs will I carry you."

It was a feature of antiquity, of ancient literature and manners, to inculcate uniform respect for the aged. Its declension in these latter days, is among the melancholy signs of the times. Once it was not only a disgrace but a crime, to fail of deference and respect to age. Now, is it not a common, and held to be a venial offence ? Is it not creeping into that dearest and holiest of earthly relations—parent and child ? And in all other relations, in all common cases, is not any high degree of respect, from the young to the old, more unusual and noticeable, than the want of it ? Is it inculcated as it was formerly in our own land ? Is it made, as it should be, a part of education, essential to good manners and good morals ? If it be not, we may have cause to remember the sad declaration, " Their is a generation that curseth their father, and doth not bless their mother." There is reason for the strong language of one, now oppressed by the infirmity but full of the peace of a good old age—"We may judge in some measure of the state of morals in any country, from the manner in which age is treated by youth. Where they, who are advanced in life, receive affection and respect, there decency is found, purity is not unknown, and the passions and appetites are under some restraints."*

Let me press the importance of this duty. Let me urge it upon those, who have the office, or in any way the control, of education. Let me press it particularly upon the regard of the young themselves. Honor the aged. Look upon age as entitled of itself to your deference. Pay it every attention, render it every service in your power. Bear with its frailties, as belonging to its condition, and coming, it may be, upon you. Let those frailties never, in their presence or their absence, be the subject of your ridicule or amusement, or that of any around you if your rebuke can silence it. Regard it as an offence against nature, decency, manners and principle. Regard the opposite, habitual respect for age, as belonging essentially to the character of a man, a gentleman, and above all, a Christian. Remember the emphatic

* Dr. Freeman, of Boston.

word of the Lord to his chosen people ;—"Thou shalt rise up before the hoary head, and honor the face of the old man, and fear thy God." Remember the terrible judgment visited upon those, who jeered at the "bald head." Be not impious mockers, but reverent helpers, of the aged. Delight to be a staff to their failing limbs, an enlivener of their solitary hours, a comforter of their sorrows. Help them to forget, not to remember, their deprivations and weaknesses. And if you are permitted to watch those weaknesses as they grow with the weight of years, to witness the decay of noble powers and the apparent withering of warm affection, if you see the inlets of knowledge and sources of common enjoyment one after another closing, if it be your privilege to walk by the aged step by step as they descend the vale—rejoice, that you can be both disciples and teachers of their waning wisdom; that you can be eyes to the blind, ears to the deaf, feet to the lame, ministers to the darkened but still eager mind, and messengers of life to the dying. * *

Powerful indeed is the appeal which comes in the broken voice of age, turning as it leaves the world to rebuke or animate those from whom it is parting forever. Most responsible the influence thus possessed, beautiful the religious use of it, melancholy beyond expression its thoughtless or corrupt abuse.

But what, (my friends of every age,) though this influence be all perverted, and the warning lost ?— What though all lips were still and all lives voiceless ? Is there not a tongue in every form that flits before us, in every change that is witnessed, in every breeze that ruffles the surface, and every storm that tosses the billows, of life's ocean ? Has not life itself always a tongue, when it comes in tremulous breathings, when it passes swifter than a post, when it vanisheth away like vapor? Do not days speak, though their possessors be dumb? And the multitude of years, shall it not of itself teach wisdom ? Look upon the aged— consider what they have been, and bear in mind, that if your most flattering hopes are granted, the change that has come upon them will come upon you, if a more fearful change come not first. A change you *will* experience, not in your bodies only, but in your minds, your views of life, your thoughts of death, your pursuits, passions, aspirations. Doubt not this, though you may strive to doubt all things else. The decree is fixed. The change is inevitable. Nature whom you may worship, has written it in every frame. History, which you trust, has told it in the swelling voice of six thousand years. Philosophy and science, in which you glory, have covered the earth with monuments to its truth. Time is already tracing it, though now perhaps with playful fingers, in your changing form and features. Every planet that flies its round, every leaf that drops, every pulse that beats at your wrist, every hair that falls from your head, tells of its coming, sure fulfilment. And before to-morrow's light lingers on the western hills, Death may inscribe it with his cold hand upon your senseless clay. "Dust thou art, and to dust thou shalt return."

AN EXCURSION DOWN NARRAGANSET BAY.

BY THE REV. JAMES D. KNOWLES.

THE morning shines in all the pride of May,
The smiling Heavens unsullied by a cloud ;
All nature hath assumed her bright array,
And wake her living choir their concert loud.
While on the deck now throng the busy crowd,
The smile of pleasure brightening every brow ;
The sails on all unfurled, the streamers proud
Sport in the breeze, and gay as childhood, now
We skim the silver wave, which sparkles round our prow.

Majestic Narraganset, o'er whose breast
  Our barque is lightly wafted by the breeze,
Fondly encircled, on thy bosom rest
  Thy nursling isles : Afar the strained eye sees,
Along thy distant banks, amid the trees
  The peasant's dwelling, where unwandering eyes,
And faithful hearts, if earth indeed have these,
  Might find that gem which fate or pride denies
To those oft envied ones, the noble and the wise.

Though never hallowed by the voice of song,
  Yet e'en here quickening recollections crowd,
Here the fierce sons of Nature held, along
  These hills and valleys, ere the forests bow'd
Beneath the white man's stroke, dominion proud :
  Wild as the cataract—whom their mother gave,
The fierce and untamed spirit which ne'er cowed
  To man, and scorning fate : But o'er the wave
The white man came—and *they* are slumbering in the grave !

Ye hapless and deluded victims—when
  Far Europe's helpless fugitives, exiled,
Fled from the presence of their fellow men,
  To seek securer refuge in the wild ;
In honest singleness of heart, ye smiled
  Upon them, and free Nature's welcome spoke,
In the heart's language, warm and undefiled :
  But soon the gathering tempest burst and broke
O'er your defenceless heads, the scathing thunderstroke.

And Philip, thou, whose name is deemed a blot
On History's page all black with human crime;
Though thou for country, freedom, life hast fought,
With spirit worthy those of ancient time:
Though wild and savage, yet thy soul sublime
Swelled high with every feeling, which could wring
The patriot's breast, who saw intruders climb
His eagle nest, and to the tempest fling
The remnant of his race, and clip his mounting wing.

Mount Hope is towering proudly as before,
The same bright smile, the fields and valleys wear,
But thou, their pride, their terror, art no more,
And thy bold followers are slumbering there:
Or haply if the battle chanced to spare
A few, more wretched, to the trackless West
They fled, to seek a refuge from despair.
Alas! the earth vouchsafes no place of rest,
Their sons are hated still, wrong'd, hunted and oppressed.

Newport! thou wast indeed a lovely spot,
Smiling in wealth and beauty o'er the bay,
Ere War despoiled thee, yet his hand could not
Sweep all thine early loveliness away.
Though Time hath written every where decay,
Still are thy hills green, and thy daughters fair;
The last rich hues of the departing day,
Full glowing on thy roofs and tall spires, there,
And fading slowly off, thy fittest emblem are.

But from the tedious dullness of thy streets,
  Which busy toil and bustle seldom cheer—
Thy mouldering wharves, which commerce rarely greets
  Or swells the tar's rude chorus on the ear—
To nature's charms I gladly turn—and here
  A scene of beauty bursts upon the eye:
Here, blooming fields and fertile hills appear,
  Below, the harbor, bay, and islands lie,
And there, the ocean rolls, wide stretching to the sky.

And here the traveller who grieves to trace
  The wrecks of former grandeur in decay,
And every heart, which loves the hallowed place,
  Which owns a fame that cannot pass away;
Must pause awhile, and parting tribute pay
  To that famed spot,* where art and nature vied,
That second Eden—but the palace gay
  Moulders in dust—neglect and ruin wide
Darken the lovely spot, erewhile the Island's pride.

GENIUS BORN; NOT MADE.

BY THE HON. THOMAS W. DORR.

THE doctrine, that the differences of talent among men are made by education and labor, in fact that "Labor is the only true Genius," seems to be gaining

* Malbone's extensive and beautiful Garden.

ground among us. The repute of this doctrine has grown out of the practical turn which every thing takes in this country ; and there are so few really great geniuses, that it is a safe one to inculcate in any part of the world excepting only the danger that it may occasionally excite an ambition disproportionate to a man's abilities, and which, with all its exertions, is destined to the mortification of having its pretensions, and even its merits disallowed.

Every young man should aim high, and then, with labor, he will become respectable ; perhaps, eminent. It is quite surprising, how great some men have become by hard study, in various literary and professional departments, whose natural powers were not above mediocrity. They enlarged by use, their acquisitive faculties to an extraordinary degree ; they may have been eminently useful, but they never became original and inventive. Let no man deceive himself with the hope of *making* himself a *genius*. This is a word of high prerogative. It indicates the possession not of any immediate divine inspiration truly, but of certain " high gifts that border on divinity," and which are not easily definable by or to those who are entirely unconscious of them. They are still, in *kind*, the same human powers which all possess in various humbler degrees, since it is the true test of genius, that its productions arrest and control the sympathies of all mankind.

Genius, in its power, is like the mysterious centre of magnetic attraction. All minds and hearts, are instinctively drawn out toward it, they know not why, and are filled with the glory and fruition of its divine works,—claiming by their very homage, kindred with its nature, and attesting by the truth and fervor of their admiration, its higher origin and nearer affinity to the

"First good, first perfect, and first fair."

This is the testimony of every age and country; and its force will not probably be impaired by any exceptions in our own. But not to be deemed too vague, let us resort to examples. If any being in this lower world is distinguished by the hand of his Maker above the rest of His intelligent creatures, it is the truly great, original, inventive, creative *Poet.* His native perceptions, susceptibilities, capacities, are different from those of common men. He sees a great deal *more* than they, in the world without; a thousand beautiful combinations, (suggesting innumerable fancies and emotions,) which are lost to the dead eye of the ordinary observer: to the favored places of the earth, where he paid homage to nature, he bequeaths associations which render them forever memorable and sacred to mankind : he perceives new, delicate, remote relations, the parents of new and striking thoughts ; he searches "dark bosoms," and unveils the mysteries of the heart and life of man ; he does not rest when he has portrayed the vicissitudes of life and the varieties of human character ; he ranges beyond the death of the body, along the endless destiny of the mind.

Further, there is no reputation so dear and coveted as that of the true poet. Other great men are occasionally remembered and admired, but the memory of the poet dwells with the noble and generous in mind, and is constantly renewed, with each rising generation, in the hearts of the young. The Temple of Fame was reared by elder hands, but the young are the guardians and patrons of its shrine. Their offerings are the richest and most sincere. The poet lives after death, on earth ; lives to the mind's eye more truly than any other man, however great his virtues, his genius, or his works. Literary men and all who have strong, ambitious minds, are well aware of this truth, and there is a wide aspiration after the fame of a poet. Horace complained in his day, of the general *rush* toward Parnassus—

> "Both fools and learned, we every where write verse."

The complaint is tenfold more distressing at the

present day. There is an unexampled competition in the poetical lists of England and our own country; yet with all the incitements of ambition, all the accumulations of classic and modern learning, all the labors of patience and industry, all the efforts of real *talent*, there has appeared but one man in this century, whose statue deserves to be placed in the temple of which we have been speaking, beside the images of Shakspeare and Milton.

But genius is not of one kind only, There are various forms of it. There is a genius of the *understanding*; and it was never better exemplified than in the mind of Newton. He is commonly cited to prove what a man of moderate abilities can do, with "patient attention and reflection." The humility of this great man, while it really favored his perception of truth, and aided his discoveries, led him to depreciate his own abilities. But it should be remembered, that when he spoke to common apprehension so poorly of himself, he was looking upward to the powers above him, and the world of truth, that lay beyond the capacity of his present limited faculties; and not downward, at the ordinary intellects and acquirements around him. The genius of the imagination is the most imposing and the most easily recognized and distinguished: but that of the understanding is not the less real. Sir Isaac had an imagination perhaps of no ordinary degree; he essayed both poetry and painting in his younger days; but his good sense told him where his greater strength lay, and he shaped his pursuits in that direction. It was the power and reach of his understanding that were so remarkable.

But, it will be asked, may not any one be an *Orator?* There is much truth in the old adage—

> "For though the Poet's born, not made,
> The Orator may learn his trade."

The first line is strictly true: any man of good talents may indeed make *verses*, and some such have more facility in rhyming than the true sons of the lyre: in other words, great numbers can and do attain to that *mediocrity*, which neither, "gods, men, nor booksellers," can endure. The second line requires qualification. Since the poets have ceased to sing their own verses, as in early times, their personal appearance and mode of speech are of little consequence, except to their immediate acquaintance. Though Dante, after the death of Beatrice, wore a savage aspect, and was fearful to look upon; his "Comedy" is not the less "Divine." Pope was none the less a poet, for resembling in his person, a note of interrogation; but his fitness for an orator, with such a figure, would have been rather questionable. It is not only necessary for the orator to have good thoughts and good words; and these are the main thing after all, but personal appearance and bearing, voice, enunciation, gesture, effect, must all be attended to, and are all to a great degree, within the reach of art. An awkward, slovenly port, (and it is of no small consequence to a public speaker how he carries himself,) may be corrected, a bad voice may be improved, rude enunciation and gesture may be amended and polished, and the orator may acquire a skill in adapting himself to his audience, to times, places, feelings, so as greatly to increase the effect of his efforts. But go into public assemblies, and you will soon learn, that all the externals of great oratory are merely accessories to something great in the mind. Suppose a man perfect in them, without strong reasoning powers and imagination, he is but feeble and tiresome. It is not uncommon, indeed, to hear speakers whose well studied delivery and gesture are so out of proportion to the littleness of their thoughts, that you listen to them with a sense of the ridiculous. Power and manner must be combined, to realize our conceptions of perfect oratory.

In truth, the really great orator is a man of genius; he is "*a poet in action.*" He is almost as rare as the poet, or philosopher of the first rank. There is a wide field for eloquence in this country; and yet, notwithstanding the amount of talent directed towards public speaking, how few decidedly powerful orators now exist, or have existed among us: and most of them have been but little indebted for their effect, to the graces of elocution. Our New-England "champion of the Constitution," has but one gesture in delivery; an awkward movement of the arms up and down, making what has been appropriately termed, with reference to him, the "lion-paw stroke." His power is in his strong vehement logic, and cold, bitter irony. Had he but a few grains more imagination—but he is great enough, too great, to be popular in this day of small men.

That there is such a thing as a natural ear for music, without which no one can be more than a mere mechanical imitator of sounds, will, I believe, be conceded by almost every one; although there may be a difference of opinion as to the defect, whether, strictly speaking, it be in the external organ, rather than in the mind itself. And will any one deny the name of genius, though of a lower form, to such divine masters as Handel, Mozart,

Rossini; who stand as far above the ordinary level of the unnumbered musical composers, as Milton, Byron, and Moore, (between whom and the artists above named, there is, perhaps, more than a fanciful resemblance,) are pre-eminent, above the ten thousand poetasters, in their several orders of excellence?

In examining the elements of a poet's constitution, we cannot fail to observe, that he must have a peculiar sensibility—a large, full heart of his own, to be able either to probe and search the bosoms of others, or to win and control their hearts, which are the depositories of his fame. These warm feelings kindle that creative faculty, by which he is characterized. We call his the genius of the imagination. I believe, also, that there is, in a very peculiar sense, a *genius of the heart.* This is a subject of itself; I am afraid to attempt it, and will leave it where it is.

Education must go on, to a certain point, nearly the same with all minds. But the time will come, and does come, in the course of mental development, when certain decided tastes and preferences are manifested in those, whatever may be their condition of life, who are destined to distinction. Consult the biography of eminent men. You do not find that early *circumstances* decided their fate; that is to say, you do not find that this man was great, or the reverse, because he was born to wealth, had every advantage of education, and was directed by anxious friends to that particular course for which they thought him best qualified ; nor that another was great, or the reverse, because he had none of these circumstances on his side. Wealth, birth, title, do not seem on the one hand, to depress and enervate the native energy of real genius ; nor on the other, do poverty, misery and neglect, seem necessary to call it into action. Where it is in a man, it will show itself, without, or against external circumstances. If Boyle, or Byron, had been born to the most squalid wretchedness, I do not believe that they would have been greater men on that account. The condition of a man of genius, may advance or retard his progress, not prevent it. We may find in the list of great men, some who were born apparently to the most unhappy fate, who never knew their parents, who were surrounded by degrading and vicious examples and bowed down by the most servile humiliation ; while, on the contrary, thousands of another sort, with every advantage of fortune and education, have gravitated toward, and at last sunk into the very state from which the first mentioned emerged. So far as I am able to learn the truth on this subject, it is, as others have found it, that ordinary men generally remain so far as their own exertions are concerned, in the conditions where the accidents of birth may have placed them; while the greater men, to whom nature has been lavish of her best gifts, vindicate their supremacy, bend and conquer circumstances, are the artificers of their own fortunes, the "sons of their own works." In the noble lines of Dryden,

> "Man makes his Fate according to his mind;
> The weak, low spirit, Fortune, makes her slave,
> But she's a drudge, when hectored by the brave.
> If Fate weave common thread, I'll change the doom,
> And with new purple, weave a nobler loom."

That genius depends on an inward impulse, and is not merely *made* by the will and exercise of the individual, is also corroborated by the fact that its possessor may for a long time give the clearest evidence of his endowment, without a consciousness of its existence. Men of powerful minds, generally find themselves out, some very early in life; but they are frequently indebted to the reaction of the popular opinion formed by their works, for the full conviction of their own superiority. It is rare for a man of genius to go through life, without expressing his love of fame, and his hope of an immortality on earth, in the memory of mankind. Milton, gloried in the assurance he felt, that he had written something which "posterity would not willingly let die." But on the other hand, is there a line in the works of Shakspeare, or an intimation in any thing which we know of his life, to show that he felt and exulted in his strength, and indulged the dream of his immortal honors. His plays are evidently written with haste and carelessness; he took no pains for their accurate preservation; and they have reached us with doubtless many additions and alterations by other hands. Shakspeare early felt

"That dear necessity of being loved;"

And although disappointed in his domestic affections, he does not appear to have resorted to those solaces of ambition and fame,

"That cheer the poverty of desert hearts."

Perhaps this absence of all affectation of a great name and of the conscious display of genius, is one of the secrets of the power of the great Poet of Human Nature.

With regard to the *labor* of men of genius: although they are not exempted from the toils of acquisition, they are above the necessity of *plodding*. They gather and arrange facts, and arrive at the conclusions, more rapidly than the generality of men. Although, a precocious memory in a child is not the best assurance of genius ; yet, on the other hand, it is true, with rare exceptions, that men of genius have great memories. They may not be idle, though their labors have not the arrangement and regularity of others. They may become slothful and negligent, and fail of attaining the just measure of their superiority ; but point out, if you can, any man of this description, whose curiosity and love of knowledge have not led him to to acquire enough to make himself known, if not so well known as he should be. Genius and acquisition naturally belong together. Milton was the greatest scholar of his age. One might suppose that Byron, if any body, lived without acquirement and study ; but we learn the contrary, from his biography. His reading was desultory, but vast. Excepting in the exact sciences, he was one of the best informed men of his day. Labor does not make the man of genius ; but he derives as much more advantage from it than others, as his native mind is greater than theirs.

But are circumstances of no account, as you before said ? the objector may ask. I did not say they were of *no* account. I said they had nothing to do with *creating* those powers of mind which are summed up in the word *genius*. Circumstances can do a great deal; they can depress the truly noble, and cover them with neglect and obloquy; they can raise the little, the sordid, the base, to high distinction, and keep them there; they can confer and take away wealth, reputation, power; they can favor or retard the advancement of those who must advance without them, or in spite of them; but they cannot make the great heart, the unconquerable will, the creative imagination, the comprehensive understanding. These divine endowments cannot be wholly concealed or suppressed; and at some time or other, in some place or other, and in some way or other, will proclaim their own majesty, and command the world's reverence. Their possessor may have been the child of misfortune and penury, from the cradle to the grave; nay, he may have perished prematurely like Otway and Chatterton, in the desperation of physical want; but if the gift of God was in him, depend upon it, there was also a record of its power, which cannot be lost, before it was taken with him to another life. The hapless son of genius, to whom fortune denied his daily bread, may make such rich provision for posterity, in his undying works, that remote generations shall call him a benefactor, and consecrate his fame. But *labor* and *circumstances* did not *make* this man.

Some one will say, it is a hard fate to which we are born; the vast majority, to mediocrity and even less. Such is our fate nevertheless. "Hath not the potter power over the clay, to make one vessel to honor and another to dishonor?" The decree of mere *power* may not justify to our minds, the way of our Maker; but if we look farther, we shall discern in this, as in all the other appointments of Providence, the purpose and the fulfilment of the greatest good. The endless variety of the natural world is not more necessary to the pleasure of the individual beings who inhabit it, than the diversity of *their* powers, conditions and employments is, to the greatest happiness of their greatest number. And after all, there *is* one great common ground of equality. The moral constitution of man, which gives him the perception of right and wrong, and makes him the just subject of a future retribution, redresses the balance of power, which might otherwise be disturbed by the preponderance of great abilities: and thus the humblest man, who enjoys an inferior portion of his maker's best gifts, may raise himself to the higher degrees of moral excellence. The duties of justice, benevolence, and piety, are common to all, because all have the power to perform them; and the worth of the performance is not measured by ability, but by the proportion between ability and its result. The sway of mere genius, without reference to its benevolent exercise, is beginning to decline, as Christianity advances ; and a life of beneficence is becoming a passport to fame. Wilberforce was blest with no genius ; but he heard the cry of the oppressed, and devoted his life and fortune to the abolition of the curse of slavery. His name will be mentioned with honor, to say nothing of future recompenses, when the names of multitudes of greater men who gratified a selfish ambition, at the expense of tears and blood to their fellow creatures, are cited with contempt, or covered with oblivion. The spirit of that great philanthropist is borne up to heaven upon the prayers of the human race. He was their friend. Let those who despair of distinction from the force of their abilities, adopt a course like his: they may be assured that there is a leaf in the Life-Book even of human memory and gratitude, for all those who dedicate their time, their talents and their substance, to increase the knowledge, the virtue and the happiness of mankind.

TIME.

BY THOMAS C. HARTSHORN.

TIME, though our friend, is often deemed a foe,
  Against him many strive with idle zeal:
The lover and the sluggard think him slow,
  And wish a rapid motion to his wheel:
While debtors, who have notes or drafts to pay,
Would gladly have him linger on his way.

The gay coquette, regardless how he flies,
  Enjoys her conquests while her charms avail,
Nor knows the truth that Flattery denies,
  Until her mirror tells the serious tale;
Then borrows she each artificial aid
To hide the ravages that Time hath made.

In vain she strives! proud monuments decay;
  Shall frailer beauty such a wreck outlive?
Alas! it is the creature of a day,
  And passes with the cloud that shines at eve,
When the bright sun in setting throws a fringe
Of rays on it—an evanescent tinge!

Nor this alone; the fairest works of art
  May fall unwept, but Genius weeps to see
The gentlest lines that ever touched the heart,
  Fade like the colors on old tapestry.

Hath he not plundered *Chaucer* of his bays,
By making obsolete his finest lays?

And *Shakspeare* too, whom Nature took to nurse
  Amid her mountain scenery, wild, sublime,
(Why did she not exempt him from the curse?)
  Hath felt the woeful ravages of Time
So much, that some think all his commentators,
Compared to Time, are harmless depredators.

The words in which they breathed their glowing souls,
  When the fine frenzy kindled up their ken,
Obscure in meaning, like the leafy scrolls
  Which zephyr wafted from the Sybil's den,
Have lost the bold conceptions they conveyed,
And given critics quite a musty trade.

Even they who led the van, and kindled war
  Along the breathing lines of clashing spears,
Have missed the fame which they contended for,
  Obscured and buried in the lapse of years;
Mentioned perhaps in some black-letter book
Covered with cobwebs in its dusty nook.

Behold what mighty changes Time can make.
  The fields that madmen fattened with their gore,
Are green and peaceful as a summer lake,
  The victors and the vanquished known no more,
Save when the sturdy ploughman, with his share,
Turns up their bones and wonders whose they were.

He who hath read the records of the past,
Perchance may recollect the cause, the date,
Wherefore and when the trumpet blew the blast
Which called these mortal remnants to their fate:
And while his soul is tuned to melancholy
He drops a tear, and sighs for human folly.

O what a tale could Time to us reveal
Of by-gone ages, when the world was new!
Thou hoary sire! thine oracles unseal!
Display thy past experience to our view!
For thou hast seen proud empires rise and fall
Before the deluge overwhelmed them all.

Thy visionary form before me now
Appears as Neptune from the main arose,
The mists of ages hang upon thy brow,
Spectres of ruined things thy train compose,
The verdure shrinks and withers at thy tread
And crowds of mortals number with the dead!

Speak while I sit submissive to thy will,
Historic truth devoid of fabrication:
I wait, with eager mind and ready quill,
To give symbolic form to thy narration.
Infuse my *ink* with all thy gathered store,
And thus from *darkness* light shall spring once more.

Tell us the story of those eastern nations
To whom the arts and sciences were known,

Ere Philip's son commenced his operations,
  Or his precursor, *Cyrus*, was o'erthrown ;
Fable sits brooding over them, and mystery
Involves the scanty records of their history.

Who reared the mounds upon Ohio's shore
  That mock research and triumph over thee !
The savage, skilled in legendary lore,
  Hath no tradition from his ancestry.
Oblivion glooms upon the buried brave
Like Desolation, on a Druid's grave.

It is imagined by the antiquaries
  That, ere Columbus found this hemisphere,
(Thou hast reduced them to these strange vagaries)
  A nobler race of men existed here.
Pray, did this race, from earthly refuge driven,
Pass with the mammoth to the Indian's heaven ?

When brilliant schemes the youthful fancy drew,
  Did after years fulfil each fond desire ?
Or did they, like the Hebrew leader, view
  Afar the consummation, and expire
Before they reached it ? Such the fate of all
Who grovel now on this terrestrial ball !

Deceitful Time ! when grief and pain annoy
  The mind and body, slow is thy career :
But when excited by some transient joy,
  Rapid thy passage through the rolling year !

Our fears, our hopes, thou bearest on thy wing,
Age's ripe autumn, and young boyhood's spring.

Even while I gaze, thou fadest from my view
As some loose cloud fantastically dight,
Which, at the evening's close, dissolves in dew,
And leaves no vestige in the starry height.
Farewell! grim phantom of an idle hour,
Which Endor's art may not to me restore!

A DEFENCE OF POETRY.

BY THE REV. DR. CHANNING.

POETRY seems to us the divinest of all arts; for it is the breathing or expression of that principle or sentiment, which is deepest and sublimest in human nature; we mean, of that thirst or aspiration, to which no mind is wholly a stranger, for something purer and lovelier, something more powerful, lofty, and thrilling than ordinary and real life affords. No doctrine is more common among Christians than that of man's immortality; but it is not so generally understood, that the germs or principles of his whole future being are *now* wrapped up in his soul, as the rudiments of the future plant in the seed. As a necessary result of this constitution, the soul, possessed and moved by these mighty though infant energies, is perpetually stretching beyond what is present and visible, struggling against the bounds of its earthly prison-house, and seeking relief and joy in imaginings of unseen and ideal being. This view of our nature, which has never been fully developed, and which goes farther towards explaining the contradictions of human life than all others, carries us to the very foundation and sources of poetry. He who cannot interpret by his own consciousness what we now have said, wants the true key to works of genius. He has not penetrated those sacred recesses of the soul, where poetry is born and nourished, and inhales immortal vigor, and wings herself for her heavenward flight. In an intellectual nature, framed for progress and for higher modes of being, there must be creative energies, powers of original and ever growing thought; and poetry is the form in which these energies are chiefly manifested. It is the glorious prerogative of this art, that it "makes all things new" for the gratification of a divine instinct. It indeed finds its elements in what it actually sees and experiences, in the worlds of matter and mind; but it combines and blends these into new forms, and according to new affinities, breaks down, if we may so say, the distinctions and bounds of nature; imparts to material objects life, and sentiment, and emotion, and invests the mind with the powers and splendors of the outward creation ; describes the surrounding universe in the colors which the passions throw over it, and depicts the soul in those modes of repose or agitation, of tenderness or sublime emotion, which manifest its thirst for a more powerful and joyful existence. To a man of a literal and prosaic character, the mind may seem lawless in these workings ; but it observes higher laws than it transgresses, the laws of the immortal intellect ; it is trying and developing its best faculties ; and in the objects which it describes, or in the emotions which it awakens, anticipates those states of progressive power, splendor, beauty, and happiness, for which it was created.

We accordingly believe that poetry, far from injuring society, is one of the great instruments of its refinement and exaltation. It lifts the mind above ordinary life, gives it a respite from depressing cares, and awakens the consciousness of its affinity with what is pure and noble. In its legitimate and highest efforts, it has the same tendency and aim with Christianity; that is, to spiritualize our nature. True, poetry has been made the instrument of vice, the pander of bad passions; but when genius thus stoops, it dims its fires, and parts with much of its power ; and even when poetry is enslaved to licentiousness or misanthropy, she cannot wholly forget her true vocation. Strains of pure feeling, touches of tenderness, images of innocent happiness, sympathies with suffering virtue, bursts of scorn or indgination at the hollowness of the world, passages true to our moral nature, often escape in an immoral work, and show us how hard it is for a gifted spirit to divorce itself wholly from what is good. Poetry has a natural alliance with our best affections. It delights in the beauty and sublimity of the outward creation and of the soul. It indeed portrays, with terrible energy, the excesses of the passions; but they are passions which show a mighty nature, which are full of power, which command awe, and excite a deep though shuddering sympathy. Its great tendency and purpose is, to carry the mind beyond and above the beaten, dusty, weary walks of ordinary life ; to lift it in a purer element ; and to breathe into it a more profound and generous emotion. It reveals to us the loveliness of nature, brings back the freshness of early feeling, revives the relish of simple pleasures, keeps unquenched the enthusiasm which warmed the spring-time of our being, refines youthful love, strengthens our interest in human nature by vivid delineations of its tenderest and loftiest feelings, spreads our sympathies over all classes of society, knits us by new ties with universal being, and, through the brightness of its prophetic visions, helps faith to lay hold on the future life.

We are aware, that it is objected to poetry, that it gives wrong views and excites false expectations of life, peoples the mind with shadows and illusions and builds up imagination on the ruins of wisdom. That there is a wisdom, against which poetry wars, the wisdom of the senses, which makes physical comfort and gratification the supreme good, and wealth the chief interest of life, we do not deny; nor do we deem it the least service which poetry renders to mankind, that it redeems them from the thraldom of this earthborn prudence. But, passing over this topic, we would observe that the complaint against poetry as abounding in illusion and deception, is in the main groundless. In many poems there is more of truth than in many histories and philosophic theories. The fictions of genius are often the vehicles of the sublimest verities, and its flashes often open new regions of thought, and throw new light on the mysteries of our being. In poetry, when the letter is falsehood, the spirit is often profoundest wisdom. And if truth thus dwells in the boldest fictions of the poet, much more may it be expected in his delineations of life; for the present life, which is the first stage of the immortal mind, abounds in the materials of poetry, and it is the high office of the bard to detect this divine element among the grosser labors and pleasures of our earthly being. The present life is not wholly prosaic, precise, tame, and finite. To the gifted eye, it abounds in the poetic. The affections which spread beyond ourselves and stretch far into futurity; the workings of mighty passions, which seem to arm the soul with an almost superhuman energy; the innocent and irrepressible joy of infancy; the bloom, and buoyancy, and dazzling hopes of youth; the throbbings of the heart, when it first wakes to love, and dreams of a happiness too vast for earth; woman, with her beauty, and grace, and gentleness, and fulness of feeling, and depth of affection, and blushes of purity, and the tones and looks which only a mother's heart can inspire;—these are all poetical. It is not true that the poet paints a life which does not exist. He only extracts and concentrates, as it were, life's etherial essence, arrests and condenses its volatile fragrance, brings together its scattered beauties, and prolongs its more refined but evanescent joys. And in this he does well; for it is good to feel that life is not wholly usurped by cares for subsistence, and physical gratifications, but admits, in measures which may be indefinitely enlarged, sentiments and delights worthy of a higher being. This power of poetry to refine our views of life and happiness, is more and more needed as society advances. It is needed to withstand the encroachments of heartless and artificial manners, which make civilization so tame and uninteresting. It is needed to counteract the tendency of physical science, which being now sought, not, as formerly, for intellectual gratification, but for multiplying bodily comforts, requires a new development of imagination, taste, and poetry, to preserve men from sinking into an earthly, material, epicurean life.

A FRAGMENT.

BY THE REV. CHARLES T. BROOKS.

"There is a rapture on the lonely shore
By the deep sea, and music in its roar:"
Thus sung the Bard; and yet he ne'er had stood
By "Purgatory,"* where its crystal flood

* Near Newport.

All green and glassy murmurs evermore,—
He ne'er had heard the music of that roar,
Nor had he heard the deep and sullen shock
Of bellowing billows at the "Sounding Rock."
He ne'er had heard the gently rippling wave
Moan o'er the pebbly flood of "Conrad's Cave."
Would he had heard these tones that he might tell
What music lingers in the solemn swell
Of the wild waves along our rock-bound coast;
How like some stern and ever mustering host,
Old ocean's billows roll and murmur here,
And greet with trumpet tones the enchanted ear.
Solemn and stately now the gathering throng
Of waves on waves deep-sounding sweep along
In measured march, far as the eye can reach
Onward they come, still onward to the beach,
Lo! in the van, with manes of flying foam,
Rank upon rank like fierce war-steeds they come,
As up the beach the snow-white lines advance
Their curling manes in the gay sunlight glance.

But ah! these words are feeble—lovely isle!
Whether the summer waves serenely smile,
Or wintry breakers dash with solemn roar
Around thy stern and wild—thy noble shore—
Thou hast a charm no pen or tongue can tell.

TRENTON FALLS.

BY THE REV. ABEL STEVENS.

Trenton Falls are in the town of Trenton, about fifteen miles in a northern direction from the city of Utica. It may seem an extravagant enthusiasm to undertake a ride of thirty miles, and that a digression from the regular route, for the purpose of seeing a single object; but no one endowed with even an ordinary love of nature will feel unrecompensed by a visit to these beautiful cascades. We started about nine o'clock in the morning on horseback. After passing through the village of Trenton, you immediately ascend a small hill, on the summit of which is a finely situated hotel, where you dismount and prepare to descend to the stream which forms the cascades.

The rivulet is called the West Canada Creek. The falls are about twenty-four miles above its confluence with the Mohawk river; they extend about two miles, and are six in number. A ridge of limestone, reaching from the Mohawk to the St. Lawrence, crosses the bed of the river through an interval of about five miles, and it is by the tortuous channel which it has worn for itself through this ridge, with the numerous precipices which its waters have been excavating for ages, that an assemblage of natural features has been produced which forms a picture unrivalled for beauty, at least in our own country.

You descend from the hotel, on the summit of the hill, a precipitous declivity, by numerous flights of steps, to the river which lies entirely concealed with overhanging forests, and is not perceptible until you step into the very ravine through which it meanders. On reaching this position, your progress is instantly arrested to gaze with wonder and delight on the scenery, beautiful beyond description, which immediately opens to your view. Above, lofty and almost perpendicular hills lift their summits upward of 100 feet, robed with thick forests until within about twenty feet of their base, where the limestone is exposed in perfect stratification, worn into a thousand varied lines of beauty, by the waters which no doubt, formerly washed them. Below, the strata extend out beneath your feet making a level pathway sufficiently wide, with the exception of occasional places where it is contracted to a few inches, and frequently projecting so far as to form large table rocks. These continued strata break nearly in their centre, affording a channel of varying width for the stream, which whirls along with great rapidity, its waters clear as crystal, now flowing smoothly like the surface of a mirror reflecting the small strip of sky perceptible above the tops of the hills and the foliage on their declivities, and then foaming over the reefs that interrupt their course, now, sweeping rapid as a lightning streak through deep chutes which they have cut for themselves, and then winding a serpentine course, in rolling eddies until they lose themselves in the distance. Now, suppose an assemblage of scenery a thousand times more delightful than this attempted description, extending for about two miles, with, at suitable intervals, six splendid cataracts tumbling over romantic precipices varying from twenty to forty-eight feet in depth, with lofty embankments, in many places projecting in threatening cliffs, under which you tremble with apprehension, and here and there large numbers of forest trees growing horizontally in their fissures, and pending over the winding waters as if charmed by their beauties, or stooping to imbibe their refreshing spray. Imagine such a scene as this fenced in by mountains from all around, accessible to the spectator only by few and somewhat difficult passages, every object shut out from the sight but the heavens above and the scenery below, where the mind can commune only with beauty and solitude—and then you may have some conception of this loveliest workmanship of nature. The prospect from any one position is of but small extent, owing to the curvatures which the stream describes among the hills. This only adds to the interest of the scenery by dividing it into a succession of pictures, each perfect in itself, and sufficiently distinguished. You may well suppose that such an interesting scene detained me the great proportion of the day, gazing and gazing again, wandering to and fro, ascending the cliffs, leaping out on the isolated rocks that lay in the channel of the stream, venturing to perilous extremities of the banks, in order to blend the feeling of the terrible with the delightful, and varying my position as much as possible, that I might catch the full expression of the scene. Never, indeed did the true idea of the beautiful more entirely penetrate my soul. I rambled along the declivities of the embankments as far as it was possible without being precipitated into the depths, sometimes standing on small protuberances not more than four inches in width, and holding on to the cliffs above, while 20 or 30 feet below, the torrent was dashing onward in its course, as a cataract sending up its thundering roar. The whole mass of limestone forming the bed and banks of the river, is full of various organic remains, some rare and valuable; indeed they seem to form the substance of the rock, for scarcely can a square inch beneath your feet be found destitute of some impression of organic existence, which in an unknown period of the past found a place of being where now rest the deep foundations of a part of an extended chasm of mountains. Thus while the whole scenery of the place renders it a beautiful and befitting temple of nature to her God, the rocky laminæ of the mountain are a record of great truths confirmatory of most important events in the providence of God, and in the narrative of his word—truths, recorded in hieroglyphics, which, after the obscurity of ages, modern science has deciphered with an accuracy almost infallible, and developed in them attestations of God's Holy Word. It may well be supposed that the Christian visitor, wandering alone amid these glorious solitudes, would catch the spirit of the scene, and, bowing on these entablatures of nature's ancient records, amid the entrancing beauty around him, send up his voice with the thunder of the cataract to Him who is God over all and blessed forever.

THE LIVING DEAD.

BY WILLIAM J. PABODIE.

"Dead men have come again, and walk about."—*Blair.*

Slam bang!—I sprang from my chair,
As springs from her form the startled hare,
When the rifle's report wakes the slumbering air.
Ghosts, hobgoblins and corpses pale,
  Witches and warlocks, Erl-kings and all
Such fancies as make up a German tale,
  And hold the soul in a fixed enthral,
Had withdrawn my mind from the world around,
And fast in the realms ideal bound,
When burst on my ear that startling sound.
I rushed to the window with fear aghast!—
'T was the slam of the blind in the nightly blast.

The night was dark, save when the beams
  Of the moon burst thro' the jagged clouds,
  Hurrying by in flying crowds,
And lit up the landscape with fitful gleams;
Or when the lightning flashed from afar,
Or athwart the gloom shot a blazing star:—
And hark to the moan of the lofty trees,
As they bend their tall tops to the breeze!

The church-yard slept in the fitful light,
And methought—was it true or fancy's flight?—
'Mid the grave-stones glimmering tall and white,

A troop of thin ghosts, like the shapes of a trance,
Were flitting about in a shadowy dance.

I rushed to the streets—the lights burned blue,—
I passed them by and onward flew,
And still I gave speed to my hurrying pace,
For methought those sprites were behind in chase.

A light gleamed forth with a dazzling glare,
From a lofty hall, on the darkened air ;
A figure stalked by me—I followed him in—
He was tall and gaunt and lean and thin—
I gazed around with a wondering stare,
And as I gazed, up rose my hair !

Some three-score shapes were seated around
That ample hall, nor breath, nor sound
Disturbed the silence so profound.
Fleshless they were, those ghastly men,
And the bone shone white thro' the o'erdrawn skin,
And O, 'twas an awful sight, to see
The deathly glare of each stony e'e !

And look ! more forms come gliding in,
Those spectral forms so tall and thin—
And the dry bones rattled, as on they passed,
Like leafless boughs in the wintry blast :—
Methought the dead had returned to life,
To revisit the scenes of their former strife.

The last had entered, the door swung to,—
I was alone with that ghostly crew ;

And O, 'twas an awful thing, to be
Alone in such fearful company !

On the rostrum now a shape arose,
Whose look my blood with horror froze ;
To his brow he lifted his skinny hand,
And glower'd around on that grisly band,
I looked as pale, I ween, as he,
When he fixed that glassy eye on me.

He comes, he comes, that fearful one !
He has left his rostrum high—
He comes !—each head is slowly turned,
And on me is fixed each eye.

I strove to rush from that haunted place,
But my limbs were smote with fear ;
I strove to shriek, but my voice was mute—
That dreadful shape was near.

He comes, he comes, that fearful one !
His breath, it fans my cheek—
'T is chill as the breeze of the polar seas,
When it blows from the icy peak ;—
His shrunken face is close to mine,
His hand is on my arm,
And his lips, those skinny lips, they move—
O God ! forfend the charm !

A voice came forth—it said to me,
" Will you join the Graham Society ?"

HENRY CLAY IN THE SENATE.

BY THE HON. JOHN WHIPPLE.

Mr. Clay had listened, day after day, with the determination to say nothing upon the subject which had been so long under debate. At last his patience became exhausted. His feelings impelled him to take the floor, and though calm, collected and full of dignity, his whole port and bearing heralded the approach of the godlike eloquence which was about to burst upon the American Senate. He rose with a sort of halo around him. Thoughts that breathe and words that burn, issued not from his lips alone, but from every attitude, every gesture, every look. It was not merely a resistless tide, a tide of power and giant strength, but a stream of glowing light, of sparkling beauty, of bewitching charms. You would have felt your hearts swelling within you, as he described the beauty and loveliness of your own, your native land. At one moment he was seen diving down to lowest depths of a clear and convincing logic ; at another soaring aloft amidst the highest heaven of pure and patriotic feeling. At one moment piercing his antagonist with the sharp edge of the keenest irony. At another, overwhelming him with the bolt of thundering indignation. Patriotism filled his heart with the warmest emotions, a clear and crystal head supplied him with the loftiest thoughts, and poetry yielded to his use her whole store of syren words, each one glittering with the rosy touch of her own heavenly pencil. On he moved in his own path of light, his country's welfare in his heart, and her standard in his hand, and he paused not, till the banner of freedom was seen floating aloft upon the ramparts of the constitution.

Let it not be supposed, that I have alluded to the brilliant effort of this distinguished man, for the mere purpose of personal eulogy. I have alluded to it as but one of the many similar efforts, some of them quite its equal, of lofty, commanding and energetic eloquence, which for the last ten years have characterized the friends of constitutional freedom in the American Senate. That little band have earned for themselves a durable and a lasting fame. For years they have stood upon the outward wall, and they have never for a moment, shrunk from the arduous duties of their dangerous position, but through good report and through evil report, they have delivered the whole word of the law, as received by them from the inspired framers of the constitution.

They have received, what to lofty and noble minds is above all rewards, the approbation of their own consciences. Some of them have fallen by the wayside, worn out in the service of their country. But many of them now live to enjoy the high reward of having imparted their own patriotic spirit to the people whose cause they have so nobly defended. That spirit it is which is now abroad in the land. It is no selfish, office-seeking spirit. It is the spirit of Brutus, which laid the imperial tyrant of Rome low in the dust. It is the spirit of Hampden, which brought to the block the head of a perjured King. Nay, it is the still loftier spirit of Washington, which awakened the energies of a great and free people, led them through a long and painful struggle, and finally crowned them with an undying glory on the heights of Yorktown. That spirit will surely prevail, for it is abroad all over the land. From the mountain tops and from the valleys of the east, upon every peak of the extended Alleghany ridge—all over the ocean-like prairies of the west, and upon every mile of the great father of waters, from the Falls of St. Anthony down to the Gulf of Mexico, the banner of freedom proudly floats aloft in the breeze of heaven. Beneath that banner, the ocean roll of this grand and glorious sentiment, is heaving and swelling over a population of fifteen millions of freeborn men.

A SEPTEMBER EVENING ON THE BANKS OF THE MOSHASSUCK.

BY SARAH H. WHITMAN.

"Now to the sessions of sweet, silent thought,
I summon up remembrance of things past."
Shakspeare's Sonnets.

AGAIN September's golden day
Serenely still, intensely bright,
Fades on the umbered hills away
And melts into the coming night.
Again Moshassuck's silver tide
Reflects each green herb on its side,
Each tasselled wreath and tangling vine
Whose tendrils o'er its margin twine.

And standing on its velvet shore
Where yesternight with thee I stood,
I trace its devious course once more
Far winding on through vale and wood.
Now glimmering through yon golden mist,
By the last glinting sunbeams kissed,
Now lost where lengthening shadows fall
From hazel-copse and moss-fringed wall.

Near where yon rocks the stream inurn
The lonely gentian blossoms still,
Still wave the star-flower and the fern
O'er the soft outline of the hill ;
While far aloft where pine-trees throw

Their shade athwart the sunset glow,
Thin vapors cloud the illumined air
And parting day-light lingers there.

But ah, no longer *thou* art near
This varied loveliness to see,
And I, though fondly lingering here
To-night can only think on thee—
The flowers thy gentle hand caressed
Still lie unwithered on my breast,
And still thy footsteps print the shore
Where thou and I may rove no more.

Again I hear the murmuring fall
Of water from some distant dell,
The beetle's hum, the cricket's call,
And, far away, that evening bell—
Again, again those sounds I hear,
But oh, how desolate and drear
They seem to night—how like a knell
The music of that evening bell.

Again the new moon in the west,
Scarce seen upon yon golden sky,
Hangs o'er the mountain's purple crest
With one pale planet trembling nigh,
And beautiful her pearly light
As when we blessed its beams last night,
But thou art on the far blue sea,
And I can only think on thee.

LAST NIGHT OF THE YEAR.

BY THE REV. EDWARD B. HALL.

Our sympathy with this hour is almost wholly retrospective. It belongs to the Past. It has little association with the morrow. The morrow has a character entirely separate—not less important, but distinct. We may not close our hearts, if they are right toward the Giver we cannot close them, to the greatness and power of a new gift of existence. We all share the natural and ever fresh joy, which an opening year awakens. But the impression is playful and evanescent, compared with the concentration and awe, with which the mind hangs upon the few, not lightly flying, but soberly moving and gazing moments of the parting season. There is power in all seasons, and all impressions are mixed. But there is one element here that belongs to no other. True, it is an association that rests upon a division of time once artificial and wholly conventional. But it has become real. And now it takes hold of the natural and the powerful. It dwells in a deep and sober conviction, that we are waiting to catch the last message, we are losing the last day, we are enveloped in the last night, of a large and marked period of that mysterious thing which we call *life* ; and of which so much is now passing into that which we call *death.* It is not the future, so much as the past, and that which is growing into the past, that here stands before us, and lays its firm grasp upon our hasting spirits, and with subdued but all the more distinct and audible accent, bids us *pause.* Time himself, the hoary and swift messenger, seems not only to stop for a moment, but even to return, and fold his wings, and walk by our side, that he may take us earnestly by the hand and discourse face to face, ere he speeds away forever.

Nor does this power of the closing year depend upon the peculiar complexion which the year may have worn to one or another. It may be affected by this peculiarity, but it does not depend upon it. He wrongs it, taking not only a selfish but a superficial view, who gives to this influence a merely personal character. Personal all influence must be, in one sense. Individual we are and human, nor from ourselves are we able, at any season, by any effort, to escape entirely. The past itself is individual to every man. Each of us, each and every one of mankind, has lived his own life. The space we are finishing has been to no two persons the same. To every mind in existence, it has been an individual and separate year. On each path it has thrown different lights and shades. To each heart that beats in the great universe of social and moral being, it has brought its own joy and its own bitterness,—with which no stranger, no friend can intermeddle. It is this thought, that gives to the present hour much of its influence. It is that its associations are individual, and yet common. None are excluded from them, and none can monopolize. No man knows that the year has been more to him than to another, in influence, instruction, or responsibility. Much as these have varied in kind, the amount may have been nearly equal to all. At least, the variation both in kind and amount has been determined more by the inward than the outward condition, and therefore has not been seen and cannot be fixed. Who can say, what workings, processes, experiences, there have been during the last year, within the breast of any one near or remote? Who can number or describe even his own? Could those of every one be recalled and revealed—all the thoughts, passions, affections, imaginations, the pleasures and griefs, that have swept over every heart, with the days and months, the meetings and partings, the gifts and losses, of the year now ebbing—could they all come thronging back upon us, and stand forth in our view, as they stand in the light of God's countenance, whatever else might be disclosed, this should we all see—that not one has reason for pride or selfishness, and not one for indifference.

Happy they "whose yesterdays look backward with a smile." The past is often present, and great is its power over every mind and heart. We cannot prevent its action, but we may profit by it. Many are they who are now experiencing its power. And with all, conscious or not, thoughtful or heedless, life is closing a solemn account. Wherever placed, however occupied, one term of probation is ending to every intelligent creature. The fact that thousands think not of it, and care not, does but deepen the solemnity of the conviction. It is still true, that to every one, on whom time has laid a light or a heavy hand, to every soul in the busy city, in the great continent, in the waking or sleeping hemisphere, another year of opportunity and responsibility has gone—yea, more fearful, is just going—is now completing that marvellous change from the overhanging, all-grasping present, to the deepening and immoveable past.

An important view of the past, urged upon us by a closing year, relates to that which men call "property." The world's moving power is gain. Man rises early and toils late, forms plans and devises implements, endures cold and heat, braves the perils of sea or wilderness, penetrates the heart of mountains, foregoes comfort, enjoyment, improvement, even character, all for property! And property, never securely held, seldom quietly enjoyed, seldom indeed, existing as a part of the present, or the past, but only of the future. And yet where is there property of any kind, either so secure or so rich, as that which the past itself offers to those who seek? Even to the mercenary, it gives that for which they should pay the debt of gratitude—its discoveries, inventions, detections, instruments and monuments. To the intellectual and moral, to the scholar, the artist, the statesman, the philanthropist, it is rich in gifts—and they may be had without price, and treasured where no moth can corrupt. All that ages have thrown up in their march, all that busy generations have accumulated and worlds brought to light, the gathered stores of centuries, the works of science, the products of genius, the results of enterprise, selfish or benevolent, the experience and wisdom of all who have ever lived—these are not merely offered, they are thrown into the lap of the present, from the overflowing past. They are forced into the paths, and hands and minds of the living. Debtors are we all, with unmeasured obligation, to the ages that have moved along, and scattered seed, and planted truths, and lighted beacons on their course. If the actors themselves who have gone with them, have not always succeeded or attempted thus to enrich those who follow, God has done it, through them, and by his great teacher, destroyer and renovator, Time. And what we may specially note is, that these gifts and influences are *ours*, in a peculiar sense. They are necessarily and indestructibly ours. We grow up in the midst of them. We are fashioned by their power. They make most of the material of life's fabric. They are clothing to the body, food to the mind, discipline for the faculties, nutriment for the whole nature. The past encircles us like an atmosphere. It wraps us in countless seen and unseen folds, its very nature enters into ours, and becomes our property forever.

This without effort. This is the appointed education and universal gift of God. Add effort, sympathy, grateful reception and discriminating appropriation—how is the gift enhanced and enlarged! He who acknowledges the Giver, and uses all powers to make the property his own not simply by inheritance but by labor and reward, becomes proprietor in the true and noble sense.

Discernment, wisdom, self-culture, and independent fidelity, will draw from the past all that it holds, and more—by blending with it the influence and original action of every free and growing mind, and all that is thus gained, nothing, nothing can take away. The treasures of the past belong to the soul.

The future is, we know not what—
  Untried, unseen, unsearchable ;
The present a contracted spot,
  Where the mind will not, cannot dwell ;
And over these is ever cast,
A blight or blessing from the past.

Delusive hope before us springs,
  Still seeking some more sunny clime,
And brings upon her halcyon wings
  Sweet promise for a future time.
That time to us may ne'er be known—
The past, the *past* is all our own.

TO SWITZERLAND.

BY THE REV. A. STEVENS.

Romantic Suisse ! still are thy memories dear ;
Thy snow-crowned peaks, thy crystal mountain rills,
Meandering midst the sloping vineyards bloom,
While blithesome songs of love and liberty
Blend with the fanning breeze and strains of birds,
And virgin hands the purple clusters pluck ;
Thy verdant vales ! with adamantine walls,
Snow-topped and reaching to the skies, fenced in ;
Sweet garden spots of earth ! with flowers decked,

While, in strange contrast, hoary winter bends,
Delayed and charmed, to smile upon the scene ;
Thy lakes, thy beauteous lakes! adorned with all
The ever-varying hues of thy glad skies—
Here shadowing forth the form of some tall cliff,
And there the vineyard's gay luxuriant growth,
While on their placid bosoms wave and glide,
Like things of air, fantastic sails of skiffs.

Sweet Leman! on thy lovely shores full oft
My youthful footsteps wandered with delight,
And oft with heart entranced reclined beneath
The shadowing mountain cliff, I drunk from thee
Delicious draughts of poetry, till thought
Dissolved away in airy reverie !
Thou art the mirror placed by nature's hand,
Reflecting back her gayest, loveliest charms.
Thy verdant shores are classic, on them roamed
The Albion bard whose reckless muse profane
Here felt thy inspiration, pure, intense,
And kindling sung in chaster, nobler lays,
Of freedom and of love, such as thine own!
The images of Julie, Clare, St. Preux
Still dwell among thy beauteous scenery.
The shades of Bonaventura, of Staël,
Of Gibbon, Fernay's patriarch, and him*
Whose thrilling pen drew lines of fire, haunt yet
Thy sylvan solitudes.

*Rousseau.

Mont Blanc!—Oft have mine eyes gazed on thy brow,
Thine awful brow! but long to gaze once more
Before they close on earth. Thou art, dread peak,
Alone, without a brother, like the God
Whose hand almighty made and holds thee up,
Sublime in thine own solitude! The storms
Pay worship round thee; winds and thunderbolts
Go from thy foot, like monarch's heralds swift,
And all the mountain tops responsive roll
Their echoing homage on, with trembling awe!
The generations of the past have gazed
On thee, but they have gone; ten thousand more
May look and die; but thou wilt still remain,—
For thou, dread genius of the mountain storm,
Shalt only sink when nature sinks and dies,
When suns go out, and stars from heaven fall.

Land of glacier and the avalanche!
Thou wert not made to be the home of slaves!
The heart among thy lofty heights beats free,
And trembles not at sceptres or at chains.
God hath ordained thee freedom's mountain home,
And built thy battlements up to his throne!
Firm hast thou stood in liberty's great cause,
Midst falling states and changing monarchies.
Still stand! stand like thine everlasting hills!
The spirits of thy Tells and Winkelreids
Are yet abroad, and thou needst never fall!

THE RELATIONS WHICH THIS COUNTRY SUSTAINS TO THE NATIONS OF EUROPE.

BY THE REV. FRANCIS WAYLAND, D. D.

THIS country is evidently at the head of the popular party throughout the civilized world. The statement of a few facts will render this remark sufficiently evident.

1. This nation owes its existence to a love of those very principles for which the friends of liberty are now contending. Rather than bow to oppression, civil or ecclesiastical, our fathers fled to a land of savages, determined to clear away in an inhospitable wilderness, one spot on the face of the earth where man might be free. *Ense petit placidam sub libertate quietem.**

2. This nation first proclaimed these principles, as the only proper basis of a constitution of government.

3. This nation first contended for these principles with perfect success. In other countries, attempts had been made to re-model the institutions of government. But in some cases, the attempt was arrested in its outset by overwhelming force; in

* The armorial bearing on the shield of Massachusetts.

others, the first movement having been succeeded by anarchy, anarchy gave place to military despotism, and this at last yielded to a restoration of the former dynasty. In our country first was the contest commenced, in simplicity of heart, for the rights of man; and when these were secured, here alone did the contest cease. Since our revolution, other nations have followed our example, and many more are preparing to follow it. But when the most glorious success shall have attended their struggle for liberty, they are but our imitators; and the greatest praise of any subsequent revolution must be that it has resembled our own. Our heroic struggle, its perfect success, its virtuous termination, have rivetted the eyes of the people of Europe specially upon us, and they cannot now be averted. To us do they look, when they would see what man can do; and while sighing under their oppressions, they yet hope to be free.

4. And lastly, our country has given to the world the first occular demonstration, not only of the practicability, but also of the unrivalled superiority of a popular form of government. It was not long since fashionable to ridicule the idea, that a people could govern themselves. The science of rulers was supposed to consist in keeping the

people in ignorance, in restraining them by force, and amusing them by shows. The people were treated like a ferocious monster, whose keepers could only be secure while its dungeon was dark, and its chain massive. But the example of our own country is rapidly consigning these notions to merited desuetude. It is teaching the world that the easiest method of governing an intelligent people is, to allow them to govern themselves. It is demonstrating that the people, so far from being the enemies, are the best, nay, the natural friends of wholesome institutions. It is showing that kings, and nobles, and standing armies, and religious establishments, are at best only very useless appendages to a form of government. It is showing to the world that every right can be perfectly protected, under rulers elected by the people; that a government can be stable, with no other support than the affections of its citizens; that a people can be virtuous, without an established religion; and, more than this, that just such a government as it was predicted could no where exist but in the brain of a benevolent enthusiast, has actually existed for half a century, acquiring strength, and compactness, and solidity with every year's duration. And it is manifest that no where else have men been so free, so happy, so enlightened, or so enterprising, and no where have the legitimate objects of civil institutions been so triumphantly attained. Against facts such as these, it is difficult to argue ; and they furnish the friends of free institutions with more than an answer to all the theories of legitimacy.

It is unnecessary to pursue this subject further. You are doubtless convinced that this country stands linked by a thousand ties to the popular sentiment of Europe. We have no sympathies with the rulers. The principles, in support of which they are allied, are diametrically opposed to the very spirit of our constitution. All our sympathies are with the people ; for we are all of us the people. And not only are we thus amalgamated with them in feeling, we are manifestly at the head of that feeling. We first promulgated their sentiments, we taught them their rights, we first contended successfully for their principles ; and for fifty years we have furnished incontrovertible evidence that their principles are true. These principles have already girded us with Herculean strength, in the very infancy of our empire, and have given us political precedence of governments, which had been established on the old foundation, centuries before our continent was discovered. And now what nation will be second in the new order of things, is yet to be decided; but the providence of God has already announced, that, if true to ourselves, we shall be inevitably first.

Now to say that any country is at the head of popular sentiment, is only to say, in other words, that it is in her power to direct that sentiment. You are then prepared to proceed with me, and remark, in the next place, that it devolves on this country to lead forward the present movement of public opinion, to freedom and independence.

It devolves on us to sustain and to chasten the love of liberty among the friends of reform in other nations. It is not enough that the people every where desire a change. The subversion of a bad government is by no means synonymous with the establishment of a better. A people must know what it is to be free; they must have learned to reverence themselves, and bow implicitly to the principles of right, or nothing can be gained by a change of institutions. A constitution written on paper is utterly worthless, unless it be also written on the hearts of a people. Unless men have learned to govern themselves, they may be plunged into all the horrors of civil war, and yet emerge from the most fearful revolution, a lawless nation of sanguinary slaves. But if this country remain happy, and its institutions free, it will render the common people of other countries acquainted with the fundamental principles of the science of government; this knowledge will silently produce its practical result, and year after year will insensibly train them to freedom.

But suppose the spirit of freedom to have been sustained to its issue, the blow to have been struck, and, either by concession or by force, the time to have arrived when the institutions of the old world are to be transformed; then will the happiness of the civilized world be again connected most intimately with the destinies of this country. Ancient constitutions having been abolished, new ones must be adopted by almost every nation in Europe. The old foundations will have been removed; it will still remain to be decided on what foundations the social edifice shall rest. From the relation which we now sustain to the friends of free institutions, as well as from all the cases of revolution which have lately occurred, it is evident that to this nation they will all look for precedent and example. Thus far our institutions have conferred on man all that any form of government was ever expected to bestow. Should the grand experiment which we are now making on the human character succeed, there can be no doubt that other governments, following our example, will be formed on the principles of right.

We have thus far spoken only of the effects which this country might produce upon the politics of Europe, simply by her example. It is not impossible, however, that she may be called to exert an influence still more direct on the destinies of man. Should the rulers of Europe make war upon the principles of our constitution, because its existence "may operate as an example ;" or should a universal appeal be made to arms, on the question of civil and religious liberty ;—it is manifest that we must take no secondary part in the controversy. The contest will involve the civilized world, and the blow will be struck which must decide the fate of man for centuries to come.

Then will the hour have arrived, when, uniting with herself the friends of freedom throughout the world, this country must breast herself to the shock of congregated nations. Then will she need the wealth of her merchants, the prowess of her warriors, and the sagacity of her statesmen. Then, on the altars of our God, let us each one devote himself to the cause of the human race ; and in the name of the Lord of Hosts go forth unto the battle. If need be, let our choicest blood flow freely ; for life itself is valueless, when such interests are at stake. Then, when a world in arms is assembling to the conflict, may this country be found fighting in the vanguard for the liberties of man. God himself hath summoned her to the contest, and she may not shrink back. For this hour may He by his grace prepare her.

THE FANCY BALL.*

BY HENRY B. ANTHONY.

As float the fancies of a gorgeous dream
That vanished with the morning's earliest beam ;
As haunts the ear some half-remembered strain
It once hath heard, and seems to hear again ;
As flowers whose beauty and whose bloom have fled,
Each bright leaf withered and each green one dead,
A grateful, an undying fragrance bear,
To tell what blushing beauty once was there ;
So turns my memory to that brilliant sight
When wit and beauty held their festal night ;
When the thronged hall its glittering groups displayed
Of nature's loveliness, by art arrayed ;
Of graceful forms that mocked the sculptor's art,
And eyes whose glances reached the coldest heart,

*Note 4.—See Appendix.

Of all that beauty loves or taste admires,
Of all that valor warms or genius fires.

First raise yon curtain; view the scenes that pass
Like shadows floating o'er some magic glass.
No canvass here, no painter tries his skill
To fix the visions that his fancy fill;
But *living pictures* fast before us rise
And *breathing* loveliness salutes our eyes.
* * * Blushing before us now
A *Novice* kneels to take her sacred vow.
Pure as the tear-drop glistening in her eye,
Fair as the roses at her feet that lie.
Close at her side a holy *Bishop* stands,
The Book of Truth spread open in his hands.
The mitred *Abbess*, bending o'er her low,
Cuts the bright tresses clustering round her brow,
And, breathing to her patron Saint one prayer,
She gives to Heaven a maid for earth too fair.

Again the scene is changed. Stern *Seyd* behold,
Flashing with gems and glittering in gold,
Fiercely on *Gulnare* turn his jealous eye,
And speak the sentence, "*Conrad* sure shall die!"

The palace fades;—the scene is changed again;
And *Conrad*, sleeping on the dungeon's chain,
Dreams of the island, o'er the deep blue sea,
Where dwell the lion-hearted and the free;
Dreams of the eye that watches every sail

To see his banner floating on the gale.
But other eyes are gazing on his sleep;
Gulnare, with purpose firm, with vengeance deep,
Bends o'er his couch, and whispers in his ear
A word, that, were he dead, he'd rouse to hear;
Raises a lamp unto his wildered sight—
Points to the dagger glittering in it's light—
And says, "I come, captive, I come to save;
Death to the tyrant! freedom to the brave!"

Behold again the curtain slowly rise,
A fairer, softer scene now greets our eyes.
Two *Lovers*, from *Albania's* classic land
Are seated side by side, and hand in hand;
She, blushing as the rose she gazes on;
He, wondering how such beauty may be won.
Her hair is darker than the raven's hue,
Her eyes as soft as Heaven's own fount of blue.
Near did Illissus' stream reflect a face
Of fairer beauty, more bewitching grace;
Nor Nymph nor Muse e'er tread, with step more light,
In *Tempe's* vale, or on *Parnassus'* height.

Next *Selim* stands and kneeling at his side,
Zuleika, blooming as an eastern bride.
Soft as the dying sunset's parting beam,
Bright as the visions of a poet's dream.

Once more the curtain raise;—be *drab* the hue;
Banish the gayer red, the gaudy blue.

Yea, verily, friend *Obadiah* see,
With broad brimmed hat, huge buckles on his knee,
Turning on *Deborah* many a loving glance,
Loath to recede, yet fearful to advance,
If outer signs the "*inner man*" can prove—
Heaven save thee, *Obadiah, thee's* in love.

The picture fades, behold another scene,
Fair *Jeannie Deans*, kneeling to England's *Queen*,
With Beauty's power, and Nature's strength alone,
Pleads for a life, far dearer than her own—
While Scotland's *Duke*, with anxious brow, stands by,
Hope in his heart, fear trembling in his eye.
Sure rarer beauty never knelt to claim
A sovereign's mercy for a sister's shame;
Fear not, sweet suppliant, banish every pain,
Such lips as thine can never plead in vain.

But hark! the music sounds, the dance! the dance!
The brilliant throngs, in glittering lines, advance—
And nodding plumes are mingling in the maze;
And knightly helmets shine and jewels blaze—
The *Brigand*, rousing from his wounded side,
Leads, in the merry reel his blooming bride.
The dark *Peruvian* and the *Naples* Maid
Fly through the waltz, or down the gallopade—
Spain's haughty *Grandee* seeks the *Gipsy Girl*,
And *Greek* and *Moslem* join the airy whirl.

Joy, joy beams bright on every face ;
And manhood's strength and woman's grace
Are here, in all their pride—
And brighter is each sparkling eye,
And on each cheek, a deeper dye,
As rolls the living tide.

From every clime where beauty smiles ;—
From *Scotia's* hills—from *Grecia's* isles ;—
From *India's* spicy groves,
From *Cashmere's* perfumed vale of flowers—
From *Russia's* snows, from *Persia's* bowers ;—
The throng of beauty moves.

With quiver o'er his shoulder flung,
And bugle-horn around him slung,
With unstrung bow and snow-white plume,
A youthful *Hunter* treads the room.
See, at his side, a *Flower Girl* stand,
A basket in her tiny hand,
With flowers of every hue—
With every leaf that's sweet or bright—
The rose's red—the lilly's white,
The violet's modest blue—
But none so sweet and none so fair,
As she, who holds the basket there !

Here stand the veteran *Sons of Mars*
Marked with the honorable scars
Of many a well-fought field.

And hearts that never bowed before,
To manhood's strength—to woman's power,
  At length have learned to yield.
The voice that paled the foe to hear,
Now whispers soft in Beauty's ear;
And Beauty's form leans light, upon
The arm that urged the battle on.

Bold *James Fitz James* and *Rhoderick Dhu*
  Meet in the circling dance;
Yet neither hostile weapon drew,
  Nor cast one angry glance.

With coat embroidered and with powdered hair,
And dress of half a century, gone by,
The master of the mansion standing there,
With right old English hospitality,
Receives each guest and bids the wine cup fly.

The Banquet comes! and the broad tables groan
'Neath the heaped luxuries of every zone;
And wines and liquors, bottled ere the flood,
Pour their rich tide and spill their purple blood.

Morning! and nothing of the scene remains,
Save the dull head-ache, throbbing in the veins.
And every bird that dared the evening blaze,
Pales it's false plumage, in the sun's bright rays,
Hunter and *Brigand, Turk* and courtly *Lord*
Doff the gay plume and lay aside the sword;

Spaniard and *Moslem* meet, to ask the price
Of cotton, "strictly prime," and "common" rice.

I saw a *Duke* and *Knight* together meet;
  Low bent the *Duke*—yet not at valor's shrine;
Down knelt the *Knight*—yet not at beauty's feet,
  But——*striving both, to pick "good fair" from "fine."*

Alas! alas! this week-day, work-day life—
  That all that's brightest, all that's noblest, best,
All that consoles us for its weary strife,
  And all that gives to time its little zest,
Should be, at most, but *fancy's* transient beam—
Fade in a *tableau*, vanish in a dream!

PHILIP OF POKANOKET.

BY GEORGE F. MAN.

To close this protracted drama so prolific in tragic incident, and worthy to fulfil the destiny apparently assigned him of becoming the sepulchre of Indian glory, now appeared upon the stage, Massassoit's second son, Alexander's brother, Pometacom or the famous Philip; a man of comprehensive vision, profound policy, enterprising genius, subtile address, lofty soul, and the keenest sensibility; one of those extraordinary characters, (met with from time to time in the history of mankind at impressive distances from each other) who are brought forward, if not wholly formed by the course of events, but, under the particular circumstances of their coming, seem expressly empowered by heaven to spread havoc and desolation, and to attest the divinity of their mission by exultingly pointing to the wounds which they sink into the very hearts of their oppressors. At a subsequent period, after the catalogue of injustice and cruelty had been greatly swollen by the English, Mr. Hubbard, the devout historian of Massachusetts, tells us, that nothing had transpired to warrant the discontent of Philip, and the historian of Massachusetts would have us believe, that the confederate colonies of Massachusetts, Plymouth and Connecticut had been lulled into the most fatal security by the peace, the harmony and feeling of brotherhood, which their mild, just, merciful, generous and disinterested policy towards the Indians had universally diffused.

The people of Plymouth, too, through their Governor, make it a matter of great merit and praise, that their solicitude for the Indians increased exactly in proportion as the objects to which it was directed were made to decrease ; that, when they had deprived Philip of nearly all his lands, they sedulously betook themselves to devising means to ensure his possession of the residue ; that, for leaving him little or nothing, he was amply compensated by the consciousness of increased security in the enjoyment of that which was left ; in short that they were at especial pains to draw around the remaining territory of this former sovereign of the forest a most beautifully constructed fence, which, though it might incidentally serve to coop Philip in, and present, in more definite outline, to his mind the image of what he had become, and, under the continuing tutelage of his protectors, might still farther expect, was wholly designed to protect him against the intrusion of the whites, or rather such of the whites as might not as wisely have considered as themselves, that there is a point of suffering beyond which endurance ceases, and as nicely weighed the farthest limits of practicable oppression.

But imagine yourself to stand where Philip stood ; to be what Philip was,—qualified by natural capacity and also from position to contemplate fully and comprehend exactly his peculiar situation, to look forward, backward, through and beyond things. Recall to mind the first coming of the Europeans, their exasperating aggressions, the depopulating pestilence which followed in their train, the arrival of the Pilgrims, their suppliance and humility in weakness, the generous hospitality which made them strong, or the kind forbearance which permitted them to become so at the hazard of its noble authors, the strength which warmed into life their injustice, their continual and never ending encroachments upon—or artful appropriations of Indian lands, incited by avarice and assisted by superior knowledge ; their gradual usurpation of power over the persons and liberties of independent nations,—with no pretext but religion, with no authority but the charter of a king beyond an ocean three thousand miles in extent, to whom these men owed nothing, of whom they had received nothing, wanted nothing and knew nothing but through the delusive tales of his grasping subjects ; the formation of treaties not understood, entered into under compulsion, and for the sole benefit of their contrivers, their arbitrary exactions under them and severe inflictions for their non-fulfilment by the Indians, their own unscrupulous violation of them, the extinction of a whole people, prefaced by the slaughter of their chiefs and the usurpation of their soil, the assumption of a wasting and harassing supremacy over the Narraganset Sachems, in return for the most generous offices, the murder of the noble Myantonomy for sheltering a fugitive from their persecution, the last days of his aged uncle, Canonicus, descending to the grave amidst his own and his people's fears, their unvarying injustice to his successors, their distinguishing favor to, open encouragement or secret abetting and support of their butcher, Uncas, the treatment of good Massassoit, Philip's father, the exasperating to madness and death, Alexander, Philip's brother ; or turning to the present and future, see Philip surrounded by living and suppliant memorials of English cruelty appealing to every sympathy that could stir a generous bosom ; the English, in spite of his remonstrance, still infusing into his people a taste for ostentation and cajoling them by traffic when force could find no pretext ; himself, in possession of comparatively a barren sceptre, the fruit of English friendship—fenced in already, and the whites still urging him, when shy, to further traffic, the fiery circle of civilization daily girting more closely its writhing victim ! And he, alas, an object of hatred for his knowledge of the past, of jealousy, for the domain he still possessed, of suspicion, for the resources his genius could still command, and the multiplied powerful motives which they had given him to put them all in requisition. See this hatred, unable to repress itself, provoking him to pursue with uplifted tomahawk into the midst of the whites, one who under their favor had dared to offer him the greatest of Indian insults, that of jeeringly recalling the name of his deceased ancestor. See this jealousy with avarice combined, forever busy in curtailing his estate, and this suspicion dogging his footsteps, and finally disarming him and his men, and declaring forfeit the weapons which their own cupidity had furnished, at a time when Indian arms had been generally disused for forty years, when the Indian chase grounds had been greatly circumscribed or mostly appropriated by the English, and one of the chief resources of Indian subsistence had in a great measure disappeared, and the attainment of what remained had been made more difficult, if not impossible, by the use of former methods of capture, in consequence of the rapidly progressing strides of the whites. Imagine Philip upon Mount Hope, revolving these things, with every billow associating some new image of grief, and calling to imagination those happier days of his ancestors when they roamed undisturbed over their wide domain and breathing every where the air of freedom, chased into toil with lusty sinew the savage inhabitant of the forest, or luxuriously reposing upon the sunny rock waited the capture of their rich repast from those yet unmolested waters.

ELEGY.

BY ANNE C. LYNCH.

THERE was no bell to peal thy funeral dirge,
No nodding plumes to wave above thy bier,
No shroud to wrap thee but the foaming surge,
No kindly voices thy dark way to cheer;
No eye to give the tribute of a tear.
Alone, "unknelled, uncoffined," thou hast died,
Without one gentle mourner lingering near;
Down the deep waters thou unseen didst glide,
With Ocean's countless dead to slumber side by side.

Thou sleepst not with thy fathers. O'er thy bed,
The flowers that deck their tombs may never wave,
To plead remembrance for thee, o'er thy head
No sculptured marble shall arise. Thy grave
Is the dark, boundless deep, whose waters lave
The shores of empires. When thou *soughtest* thy rest
Amid their silent depths, they only gave
A circling ripple, then with foaming crest
The booming waves rolled on, o'er their unconscious guest.

'T is said, that far beneath the wild waves rushing,
Where sea flowers bloom and fabled Peris dwell,
That there the restless waters cease their gushing,
And leave their dead within some sparkling cell,
Where gems are gleaming, and the lone sea shell
Is breathing its sweet music. And 't is said
That Time, who weaveth over earth a spell
Of blight and ruin, o'er the Ocean's dead
He passeth lightly on, with trackless, silent tread.

Then, though no marble e'er shall rise for thee,
No monument to mark thy last, long home,
Thine ocean grave unhonored shall not be.
The coral insect there shall rear a tomb
That age shall ne'er destroy ; and there shall bloom
The fadeless ocean flowers. And though the glare
Of the bright sunbeams ne'er shall light its gloom,
Yet glancing eyes and forms unearthly fair
Shall throng around thy couch, and hymn a requiem there.

Now fare thee well ! I will not weep that thou
Didst pass so soon away ; for though thou wert
Still in thy boyhood's prime, and thy fair brow
Undimmed by care ; yet sad was thy young heart,
For thou hadst seen thy light of life depart,
And Love had thrown a wild and burning spell
Around thee, and with sly insidious art
Had maddened thee. Then sounded loud the knell
Of all thy bright young dreams. My earliest friend, farewell !

GO FORTH INTO THE FIELDS.

BY WILLIAM J. PABODIE.

" The world is too much with us."—*Wordsworth.*

Go forth into the fields,
Ye denizens of the pent city's mart!
Go forth and know the gladness nature yields
To the care wearied heart.

Leave ye the feverish strife,
The jostling, eager, self-devoted throng ;—
Ten thousand voices waked anew to life,
Call you with sweetest song.

Hark ! from each fresh clad bough,
Or blissful soaring in the golden air,
Bright birds with joyous music bid you now
To spring's loved haunts repair.

The silvery gleaming rills
Lure with soft murmurs from the grassy lea,
Or gaily dancing down the sunny hills,
Call loudly in their glee !

And the young wanton breeze,
With breath all odorous from her blossomy chase
In voice low whispering, 'mong th' embowering trees.
Woos you to her embrace.

Go—breathe the air of heaven,
Where violets meekly smile upon your way ;
Or on some pine-crowned summit, tempest riven,
Your wandering footsteps stay.

Seek ye the solemn wood,
Whose giant trunks a verdant roof uprear,
And listen, while the roar of some far flood
Thrills the young leaves with fear !

Stand by the tranquil lake,
Sleeping 'mid willowy banks of emerald dye,
Save when the wild bird's wing its surface break,
Chequering the mirrored sky—

And if within your breast,
Hallowed to nature's touch one chord remain ;
If aught save worldly honors find you blest,
Or hope of sordid gain ;—

A strange delight shall thrill,
A quiet joy brood o'er you like a dove ;
Earth's placid beauty shall your bosom fill,
Stirring its depths with love.

O, in the calm, still hours,
The holy Sabbath hours when sleeps the air,
And heaven, and earth decked with her beauteous flowers,
Lie hushed in breathless prayer,—

Pass ye the proud fane by,
The vaulted aisles, by flaunting folly trod,
And 'neath the temple of the uplifted sky,
Go forth and worship God!

LIBERTY'S TREES.

BY THE HON. JOSEPH L. TILLINGHAST.

(Written early in 1812, in prospect of hostilities with France or England.)

O leap from the mountain, thou firm rooted Oak,
And shake off thy vesture so grand,
Yield thy rugged old limbs to the architect's stroke
And sweep from the foam-whitened strand.

Down, down from thy highland, thou winterless Pine,
O cast thy green mantle away;
Thy head—with the streamers of war let it shine;
Thy breast—let it dash the storm-spray.

Trees hallowed and sacred! Full long have your brows
In Heaven's golden lustre stood shining;
While shaded, beneath, by your balm-breathing boughs,
Religion and Peace were reclining.

And oft in the tempests of vengeance and power,
Your bosoms the glebe have defended;
And oft on your heads, that still steadily tower,
The shaft due to man has descended.

Now leave the old mountain all bare to the storm
And let the free bolt 'round us roll;—
The tempest can only our bodies deform,
But servitude killeth the soul!

See o'er the red wave, ever blushing with gore,
False Gallia her pennons advancing;
Beneath the dark Eagles so ruthless that soar
How the eyeballs of Rapine are glancing!

Beyond, see old Albion her War-Cross display
Both the Free and their foe to appal—
As the lion and panther contend for their prey,
So the Briton and Frank for our fall.

Ye Cedars, ye Firs, that the torrent floods lave,
Descend from the heights ye adorn;—
In the cloud of your canvas, far-shadowing the wave,
Be the thunder of Liberty borne!

Rush, rush, thou warm blood through the veins of our youth,
And, while their swoln bosoms are beating,
Let them strike, and strike firmly, for Freedom and Truth,
One blow, that may need no repeating!

Then hail to the years that in honor shall flourish
When glory and safety combine;
Once more, grassy hills, 'mid the bowers that ye nourish,
Religion and Peace shall recline.

PERRY, ON LAKE ERIE.

BY THE HON. TRISTAM BURGES.

Commodore Perry arrived at Erie on the 26th of March, 1813. He carried with him from Newport, 149 men and three boys, all of whom were volunteers.

The fleet of Eneas, so Maro sings, when riding at anchor in the Tyber, and, in his absence attacked by the Rutulians, and likely to be burned, was, by a miracle of poetic mythology, changed into a shoal of dolphins, and went off sporting down the stream; and if so, they may, for aught we know, be at this time playing about the mouth of that river; or showing their bright sides to the sun, in other parts of the Tyrean sea.

Perry and his hardy Rhode-Island mariners, travelled up to the lake, for something not quite so poetic.

They were required to change the oaks, and the green pines and hemlocks, then standing on those shores, into a fleet of ships and vessels, and fit them out to encounter, and overcome, in battle, on those waters, a fleet then armed, equipped and manned with British sailors; men, who had never, before that time, met an equal, in any fleet, on that element.

In this there was no poetry, nor any other miracle than bone labor, matchless skill, and unconquerable bravery.

Every Yankee is an axe man; and all the companions of Perry were of the full blood; and most of them the best of that blood, the Rhode-Island stock.

These, with a few more shipwrights, smiths, caulkers, riggers, and sailmakers, built and equipped this fleet; and launched the whole into the harbor of Erie, rigged and ready to sail, in about ninety days, after the first blow was struck.

They built from the stump, six vessels; the Lawrence, of twenty guns—two long twelves, and eighteen 24 pound carronades; the Niagara, of two long twelves, and eighteen 24 pound carronades; the Ariel, of four guns, 18's and 24's; the Scorpion, of two guns, thirty-twos; the Porcupine, of one gun, a thirty-two; and the Tigress, of one gun, a thirty-two.

During the same time, they repaired and made efficient, the Caledonia, of three guns, 24's and 32's; the Somers, of two guns, thirty-twos; the Trippe, of one gun, a thirty-two, and the Ohio, of like force, but not in the battle.

At the mouth of the harbor of Erie, there is a bar; and on this, the water was then so shallow, that the vessels could not be *floated* out over it. They had been built in this place, because, in no other on the lake, could they be secure from the enemy.

To carry them out over the bar, in the face of this enemy, superior in force, had they all been furnished with guns, and, as it must be, entirely unarmed, was a labor which tasked the Yankee invention, no less than the valor, of the young Commodore and his associates.

They were loaded on the backs of camels, and carried out over the bar into deep water. An Arab, who, from the back of his camel, on the desert, had, at a safe distance, looked at the French and English fleets, in the bay of Abouker, would not believe a word of all this story.

It is literally true. These camels were of simple mechanism, and American manufacture. They were long, broad, deep boxes, made of planks, like scows, and perfectly water tight; with holes to fill, and sink, and pumps to exhaust them of water, and raise them so as to float with their upper edge high above the surface. These, placed on each side, and connected by strong beams, on which the vessels being placed when they were sunk; thus raised the vessels up above the bar, when the camels were pumped out, and rose again by their own buoyancy.

The guns of the fleet had been mounted in batteries on the shore; and the militia, under General Mead, then encamped in the neighborhood, were embodied, and united with the seamen in defending these vessels, while they were thus travelling over the bar, on the backs of these able bodied camels.

Thus, in the face of an enemy, superior in force, this fleet was built, put afloat, and equipped. The enemy, however, before they were ready to make sail, withdrew to the harbor near Malden; and retired under the guns of the British fortress.

The British vessels were stout built, with thick bulwarks of solid oak; but the American were built in a hasty manner, and intended merely to carry guns and men; and bring them down along side of their adversary.

How long the British fleet might have kept their shelter, in the harbor of Malden, is not known. Exigences called them out; the want of provision, in the British army, compelled them to put out, and attempt to clear the lake of the American fleet; so that they might, with safety, run down to Long Point, their depot of stores, and provision the camp.

The British fleet had a *veteran* commander, the American, a *young* sailor. Barclay had *conquered* with *Nelson*, at *Traffalgar*; Perry had probably *never seen* the combined movement of ships, in a fleet, formed in line of battle.

The two fleets might be equal in number of men; but all, in the British, were seamen, or marines, or soldiers; while many, in the American, were militia, or new levies, from the ranks of the army.

In number of vessels, we exceeded by three; the enemy had a superiority of ten in the number of guns. The vessels of the enemy were impervious to the shot of our carronades; but their long guns hulled the thin sides of our vessels, through and through. Let Him be praised who has told us that "the battle is not always to the strong."

On the night of the 9th of September, 1813, the American fleet lay moored at Put-in-Bay, on the southwest shore of Erie. At daylight on the 10th the enemy were discovered from the mast head of the Lawrence, far up the lake in the northwest. This was, by signal, immediately communicated to the fleet; and, at the same time, the signal was given to get under weigh.

Commodore Perry, soon after, hoisted his broad pennant on board the Lawrence, inscribed with the immortal words of him whose name his vessel bore—"*Don't give up the ship.*" And at the sight of it, the loud huzzas of the mariners resounded over the lake, from deck to deck, along the whole American line; and awakened the echoes which had been sleeping on those waters and shores, ever since the morning stars sang together.

The breeze being light, the American fleet was two hours in bearing down under all sail over this smooth surface of nine miles. The wind, though light, was steady; and not a new movement was made in steerage, running geer, or sail. All were silent. It was, in both fleets, the stillness of the elements, before the storm of the hurricane. I will not believe one bosom palpitated with fear; but many a one beat with an aspiration, and a hope for victory. In that awful pause, when at times, every eye glanced on every other eye, and all were mingling souls in a sympathy of courage and daring among their comrades and commanders, how many young hearts, for the last time, breathed a sigh and prayed a prayer, for home, parents, brothers, sisters, and for "the bosom friend dearer than all?" Many a bright and moist eye looked, for the last time, on the green shores and sunny hills of their country. Rashness, without courage, may rush thoughtlessly into the battle; but nothing but valor of soul can stand unmoved, and wait for the coming conflict of life or death, victory or defeat.

They stood every man silent at his post; while the breath of heaven, born to fill the sails of commerce, and which never had before, seemed reluctant now, on those quiet waters, to aid men in mutual destruction. * * * * * *

At the close of the battle, Perry set up no *exclusive* claims to the glory of the victory. He submitted all, with unexampled modesty, to the award of his country.

Look at his despatches; does he tell what *I* have done? To General Harrison—" *We* have met the enemy, and they are *ours*." To the Secretary of the Navy—" It has pleased the Almighty to *give* to the arms of the United States a signal victory over their enemies on this lake. The British squadron consisting of two ships, two brigs, one schooner, and one sloop, have this moment surrendered to the force under my command, after a sharp conflict."

Nothing can be so conspicuous as the modesty, unless it be the piety, of this most perfect of all naval despatches. How could he say less of himself? The victory had been given by Him who gives all things—had been given, not to him, but to the *American* arms. The British squadron had surrendered to *the force*; what force? He could not avoid saying, to the force under *my* command. *One* epithet only, tells the nature of the battle; it was a *sharp* conflict. He puts under sail none of that *squadron of adjectives*, after which, a young egotist would have sent his first victory to the Naval Department.

The living can protect their own characters. Those who are dead, and who fell in the national service, have left their fame, perhaps the only inheritance of their children, to the safe keeping of their country; and wo betide a people, when they permit the sanctuary of human glory, frail and perishable as it is, to be *profaned* and *plundered*.*

It was sacrilege among the ancients, and deemed abhorrent to gods and men, to destroy, or remove a stick or a stone, from a trophy erected, by a conqueror, on a battle field, or by the shore where a naval victory had been achieved.

Let the people of Rhode-Island protect with a pious diligence, the tombs and the glory of their buried patriots and heroes; and alike abhor those who would tarnish the one, or demolish the other.

*Note 5.—See Appendix.

THE DWARF'S STORY.

BY FRANCES H. WHIPPLE.

"Nay, listen to me, Lilian ! I 'm not mad.
Linger and listen. I would tell a tale—
Oh, God ! sustain me !--but 't will wring thy heart,
I would not grieve thee—thee, my only friend !
But yet I cannot—how can I forego
Thy precious sympathy ? Give here thy hand ;
I 'll hold it thus in mine. There, turn away,
And look not on me ; for I cannot bear
That thou should'st feel disgust—that thou should'st loathe,
Though the sharp hiss of universal scorn
Has been my only greeting from the world.
Lilian, thou hast dear woman's gentleness,
Without her vanity. O, thou might'st lead
The noble and the great in pleasant thrall,
Casting such chains as men delight to wear ;
Yet, dearest, thou art mine--the friend of him
Who has no other. Yes, I owe thee much."

"Thou ow'st me nothing. Mine--all mine the debt !
Do I not owe thee all I value most—
Treasures of intellect, the wealth of mind ?—
What had I been this moment, but for thee ?
O, cold will be this heart ere I forget
My endless debt of gratitude and love !"

She turned her blue eyes on him, with the tears
Softening their lustre, like the pearly gems
Of dew in violets. The little hand
Trembled within its confines. One low sigh
Escaped his quivering lips.

"Dear girl, beware.
Reprove, condemn, or scorn me ; but do not,
For my sake and thy own, O do not be
Thus kind, thus gentle, or I shall forget
My vow of fealty. Yet leave me not ;
And fear me not. Within this shapeless clod
A spirit dwelleth, fervid, pure, and high,
As thy own spotless one. It loveth thee
And cannot do thee wrong—would not for worlds.

"Be calm and hear me dearest Lilian.
A living curse I came into the world ;
And when I was an infant—ay, a babe,
My little, hideous, melancholy face
Drew nought but hatred on me. Then I learned,
Ere I could syllable the simplest word,
The worth of beauty ; for I saw it give
All that a child desireth unto him,
My bright eyed brother. He was beautiful.
My mother loved him ;—but she hated me !
I 've seen his dimpling arms around her neck ;
And, looking on him, her expressive eye
Was one rich gush of love! Then how I longed

To cling there too, and share her dear embrace !
But, oh, if I drew near, a cold repulse,
A loathing look, a shudder of disgust,
Told me how dear I was. Yet, even then,
My heart was burning, bursting with its love,
That yearned to gush, nor asked a meet return.
But nothing loved me. My old ugly nurse,
The dogs, the horses ; yea, the very cat,
Read in my crouching brow—my skinny limbs,
The brand of hate, and loathed the cursed one !
Even when a child I prayed, I longed for death !
The grave could have no terror ; and the worm,
With all its slimy length twined in my hair,
Or knotted in my bosom, could not loathe
The form he feasted on ; and this was joy !
The noisome reptile seemed to me a friend !

"O, dry thy tears, dear Lilian ! Do not weep !
I cannot bear to see thee weep for me !
I envied every thing, for nothing lived
Cut off from love and its sweet fellowship,
With one accursed exception ! The poor moth
That fluttered for an hour, and then was gone,
Had brethren like itself. The vilest thing
Knew kindred, and the claims of kindred love !
There was an idiot child, inert as clay,
I envied for his very senselessness,
And wildly prayed that I might be like him !
O, had I met one kind, one gentle look,

One token of affection, I had been
Happy despite my fatal ugliness ;
And I had loved with more than human power !
But crushed affections petrified within ;
And all my latent love to hatred turned,
Creating gangrene to corrode itself.

" The measured wrath not yet had touched the brim.
Heaven gave a little sister. Months went by,
I durst not look upon her. She was kept
Far from the frightful monster. Still I caught,
At times, a passing glimpse. How fair she was!
Her little cherub form—her silvery voice—
Her thousand beauties—thousand witcheries—
Mocked me with all their loveliness ; and then
My spirit's venom took a bitterer depth !—
I hated her !—I hated that fair child
With half a thought of murder ! But, at length,
One pleasant eve, as little Marion sat
Twining her fingers in the chesnut curls
Of my fair brother, in her gleeful sport
She pulled the silken mesh. Enraged with pain,
He flung her, screaming, on the marble floor !
She looked to me for comfort—looked to *me!*
Merciful God ! I thank thee, even now,
For but the memory of that blessed look !
I clasped her in my arms. She clung to me.
She laid her cheek to mine ; and, sobbing low,
She murmured, in her sweet imperfect way,

The name of *brother!* Nature taught the word;
How, else, could she have given the name to me?
The flint burst quick within me and the ice
That lay beneath was melted into tears.
The gushing torrent checked me.

"Need I tell
How day by day she loved me? How I lived
Like one awaking from a horrid dream—
Waking to life, and happiness and love?
They could not tear her from me. Gratitude,
Or cherub pity for the hated one,
Made that angelic spirit all my own.
I only lived when with her—only slept
That I might dream of her. A thought of death
Would sometimes cross my brain and madden me!
The augury was prophetic. She grew ill.
I watched by her. I never left her couch
For one long, awful week—and then, she died.
The light of my existence was put out!
The living fountain of my desert failed!

"My former bitterness with awful strength
Gathered back its tide, and overwhelmed my soul;
And festering deep within the sorest part,
The venom lay of disappointed hope:
And then the beaker of my lot was full!

"I watched the body. None could tear me thence.
When none were by to blame, or to forbid,

I took her from the coffin, held her close
Within my flaming bosom, with a hope
Its fever yet might warm her. All in vain,
No single tear relieved me. Back I laid,
For the last time, my treasure ; and sat down
With all the silent firmness of despair.

"I begged—I prayed in vain. They buried her.
Night after night, and day by day, I watched
Beside the lonely tomb. At midnight deep
I called to her, entreating for one word !
I made the silence vocal with my cries!
And then I listened—listened without breath,
For the dear name of brother ! O, I thought,
Might that one word be whispered from the grave,
I could go back and be at peace again !
But echo mocked me, as I called her name!
The deep shades mocked me, and the placid stars ;
The cold earth mocked me, and the heartless moon !
All nature mocked me. Nothing, nothing knew
What the heart suffers that has lost it's all !

"Insanity relieved me ; for my brain
Was touched with raging fever. But I rose
From my lone couch of bitter suffering
With a new purpose graven in my soul.
I had the spell of genius. Fame had called.
I heard her syren voice, and vowed a vow
To be what men adore ; and thus avenge

The shapeless body, through the o'ermastering mind!
Then silently I turned away, and bound
My soul to its grim purpose. Long, long years,
Of deep, intense, unceasing study, wrought
With the quick fires of genius, gave a name
Emblazoned with the loftiest—WON THE MEED!

"I wore my triumph proudly, for a while;
But when I longed for kindness, then I found
Fame, honor, glory, could not purchase love!
My reputation was an ice-berg, high,
Magnificently cold, unenvied, lone;
And in the splendid panoply I stood,
As a volcano 'neath a frozen sea.

"I left my native land, and wandered here:
Then, on the darkness of my being, rose
The lovely morning star. O, need I say
Whence came that thrilling heart-beam? Lilian
I need not tell thee how my buried love
Warmed into being, lived again in thee;
Yet chastened by a sorrowful mistrust
Of its endurance—by experience taught!
O, hadst thou been as shapeless and deformed
As this vile clod, how madly could I love!—
Ay, worship thee—hoping for love again!
But, now, endearing as thou art, and kind,
I wrong thee not—I know thou canst not love.
'T is well. Hark, hark! Didst hear a thunder tone?
It comes! 't is coming! This is my last hour!"

"Oh, no! what meanest thou? It cannot be."

"Peace, dearest Lilian. Listen yet again.
When I am gone, and thou dost wander here,
At eve, or morn, or the deep stilly noon,
Then think of him who woke the latent springs
Of genius in thy soul; of him who led
Thy spirit from the shadows, giving thee
Sources of pleasure thou hadst never known.
Think of him then, beatified, and pure,
An angel presence, beautifully fair,
Waiting in some sweet bower of Heaven for thee!
Thus shall it be, my Lilian. We shall wed.
Our God shall join our spirits; and the lyres
Of cherub, and of seraph, shall be swept
To gladden our espousals! O, I know
We shall be wedded for eternity;
And, hand-in-hand, and soul inwrought with soul,
We shall advance forever, finding out
The living waters through the maze of love,
And light, and music, that make heaven, *Heaven,*
With such a gush of worship on our lips
As may wake angels to new songs of praise!
Look to this hope, my Lilian, and I know
My memory shall live within thy soul,
Like a shrined presence, where affection still,
May minister, and hold communion sweet!
I know thy gentle nature. Kind and true
Will be the tears thou givest. Weep not long;

But go abroad, and con my lessons o'er.
The flowers, the rocks, the stars, the clouds, the dews,
Are living with them. Ponder on the laws
That animate, and govern, and sustain;
And thus remember me, but not with tears.

"Again that thunder! I have had a dream—
A horrid dream! That vivid flash again!
The scene, the hour, were such as even now
Are round and o'er us. Hither then we came;
And we did sit as now; one gentle hand
Pressed fondly thus in mine. Nay, tremble not.
This lofty elm, those venerable oaks,
Hung their rich shade below. The laughing brook
Was gurrulous and clear; and as light clouds
Passed o'er the sunshine, shadows swept along
O'er the swayed grass as coolingly as now.
A cloud came up and blackened suddenly—
Like yonder frowning one. O, leave me not!
I told the tale I 've just related thee;
And one bright tear stood in thine either eye;
One yellow curl, like this, was on thy neck;
Thy drooping eyelids fell, as now they fall;
Thy soft, transparent cheek was pale and cold;
And thou wert sweetly beautiful, as now!
I held thee to my bosom. Nay, shrink not,
I'm telling thee a dream! My yearning soul
Exhaled itself in one long, frantic kiss!
Thus, even thus, my lips were joined to thine!

A horrid flash (like that!) it blasted not!
And yet I fell. I felt thy fingers press
Upon my eyelids! Lilian! Lilian! Oh!—
Great God! forgive me!—Lilian! Water!—"

* * * * * * * * *

The lightning had not touched him; but he lay,
Low at the feet of the distracted girl,
A livid corse; thus yielding up to her
The highest sacrifice of love—a heart
That could not prove its worth, until it broke!—
And yet that shapeless being had a mind
To pierce the deepest mystery—a heart
That might have won an angel from its sphere!
He walked alone amid a world of love,
Dying for what is wasted; like the wretch,
Stricken with pestilence, who lays him down
In nature's loveliest bower, where waters play
Almost within his touch. The cooling splash,
Mocking his thirst to madness, still he hears!—
Oh, aggravating torture, thus to die!—
While floods are round, to perish for a drop!

EXTRACT FROM A POEM.

BY THOMAS A. JENCKES.

If no true spirits there were left to guide
The trembling state o'er factions stormy tide,
If no tried steersman seize the rocking helm,

Shun the wild waves that threatening yawn to whelm ;
If from this fount the stream of poison steals
Through all the nation loves, or thinks, or feels ;
Beware, proud Union, though thy power and wealth
May gild the ills that mine thy public health.
Though 'neath thine eagle flag, proud navies ride,
Where winds can waft, or ocean heaves his tide,
Though still thy call the patriot's heart should warm,
Fire the true soul, and nerve the sinewy arm,
Though from each mountain height to ocean wave
Swells the deep anthem of the free and brave ;
Yet could these save thee, when the poison's course
Shall taint with death, thy life-blood's inmost source ?

So thine own bird, the warrior Eagle, nurst
Where rolls the avalanche, and thunders burst,
Soared from his mountain eyry, free and high,
And thousands watched him wheeling through the sky ;
Upward he sprang exulting on its flight,
Then paus'd and fluttered—from his cloudy height
Men saw his fall, and wonder'd as they gaz'd ;
No bolt was sped—no blasting lightning blaz'd,
The secret viper curled beneath his wing,
Poison'd the life blood in his heart's warm spring,
Sank the proud bird, once monarch of the skies,
His dying hymn the raven's funeral cries.

Yet fear we not—a bold and Spartan band
Rise firm midst them whose contests shake the land,

We trust a power above all rulers' art,
The power that guides to truth the human heart ;
And while yon eagle standard floats, and thrills
The heart that's nurtured on our own free hills,
No power but heaven, no victor but the grave,
Can crush that band, omnipotent to save !

SONG OF THE WINDMILL SPIRITS.

BY ALBERT G. GREENE.

Ha, ha !—here we are, and the moon has not set ;
And the mossy old Windmill is standing here yet.

The harvest is gathered, the summer has gone,
And again we rejoice in the scent of the corn.
Up all,—to the wings now ! blow high, or blow low,
Round on the old Windmill once more we will go !
The trees have been leafless, their branches all white,
Since we left it, last autumn, one cold, frosty night,
And went far away from the region of snow,
To see the magnolia and locust-tree blow :
Then, the warm, sunny fields of the south we have trod,
To see the white cotton burst out from its pod ;
And then, far away to the bright torrid zone,
Where the orange, and lemon, and citron have blown.
But once more, the season we love has come round,
And here, to enjoy it, again we are found ;—
And while the bright moon which now lends us her beam,

Is looking alone on the rock and the stream,
And gently the dews of the midnight distil,
We will have one more ride on the wings of the mill!

Stretch out, then stretch out, to the end of each wing,—
And send them all round, with a good, hearty swing;
Up and down—up and down—send them merrily round,—
Bear them down on that side, from the sky to the ground:
Now up!—send them up:—on this side let them fly
With a bound from the ground, till they point to the sky—
Now they crack: never mind,—they are used to the strain:
Up with them once more,—now down with them again!

How gaily, that morning, we danced on the hill,
When we saw the old Pilgrims here building a mill;
There, at day-break, we stood when they laid the first stone,
And came, every night, till their labor was done.
How often around its old wings we have hung,
And have gambolled and laughed, and have shouted and sung.
Its frame-work all fell, ere a century waned,—
And only the shaft and the millstones remained.
It was built all of wood,
And bravely had stood,
Sound hearted and merry as long as it could:
And the hardy old men
Determined that then
Of firm, solid stone they would build it again,
With a causeway and draw,
Because they foresaw

It would make a good fort in some hard Indian war.
But they all are gone, its old builders are gone,—
They are all in their graves and a new race is born :—
All, all of its builders,—the head which had planned,
Each hand which helped raise it, each honest old hand,—
They are gone, all are gone,—all are low in the mould,
And the new mill itself is an hundred years old,
But still, when the harvest has been gathered in,
Up here in the moonlight we always have been ;
In the soft autumn midnight, still, year after year,
The wind and the moonlight have found us all here.

But when the frost comes and the sleet and the snow,
And the green leaves are dead, then far southward we go,
And rove 'mid the rich fields of rice and of cane,
Till the bright northern summer recalls us again.

We love the clear breeze o'er the pine covered hill,
As it sings through the wings of the sturdy old mill.
There it comes ! now spring out to the end of each rail,—
And let each arm bend like a mast in a gale.
Round with them,—round with them,—the wind is too slow,
Bear down all together, hallo ! there, hallo !
Fill the hoppers below—heap them up till they choke,—
And let the old stones then fly round till they smoke.
Round, round, send them with a merry good will ;
Ha ! ha ! we are back to the rattling old mill.

And Ephraim, the miller, the drowsy old head,
Who lies now at midnight asleep in his bed,

Should he wake, would suppose
That because the wind blows,
And for no other reason,—around the mill goes,—
When, at sunrise, he comes, and our work he has found,
How little he 'll know how his grist has been ground,—
Then, round,—send it round!—for our work must be done
Ere old Father Ephraim appears with the sun.

Though fair are the plains of the south and the west,
We love the green fields of New-England the best.
For here, while we see o'er the golden-edged plain,
Each low, fertile hillock all waving with grain,
We know, that rewarding its patience and toil,
The hand of the free reaps the fruit of the soil.
We are free as the blue air around us is free,—
And so we would have all God's creatures to be.

Ha, ha! a fresh breeze now comes over the hill:
Each sail feels its breath:—now they stiffen and fill!
Now, now, all is straining above and below,—
And round the quick circle we merrily go:
Round, round,—and now hark to the musical tones
That come quivering out from the whirling old stones!
What joy can compare
With the life that we bear:—
The earth is our play-ground, our home is the air.
How happy are we,
How happy are we,
'Midst the beautiful things of the land and the sea.

When the moonbeams fall clear, through the silence of night,
And the dew-drops are sparkling like gems in the light,
We love, bounding forth with the speed of the gale,
The rich, teeming cornfield's sweet breath to inhale;
While each stalk gently bends, as they bear us along,
And waves its green arms in response to our song,
And the spindle's tall plume that droops over its head,
Just moves in the air, as it springs from our tread.

And when our gay revels have drawn to a close,
'Mid the cool, verdant foliage, how sweet to repose:
Or to rock in the leaves, when all round us is stilled,
And commune with the life with which nature is filled,
Which above and below,
Forever doth flow
Rejoicing around us, wherever we go,—
And to mortals unknown,
To us hath been shewn
By Him who made all and who sees all alone.

How often we listen delighted, to hear,
Beside the green folds of the delicate ear,
The voice of the tender young mother of corn
Singing 'mid her fair brood which within it were born,
While breathing in fragrance and cradled in silk,
They are drawing forth life from her fulness of milk.

And when the bright days of the summer have fled,
Its beauty all withered, its verdure all dead,
The care and the toil of the season all past,

And the full, golden harvest is gathered at last,—
When the gay, merry groups to the husking repair,
'Though unseen and unheard, yet we often are there.
While the chinks of the barn are all streaming with light,
And sounds of loud glee wake the echoes of night,
Our voices prolong
The laugh and the song,
And answer each shout that bursts forth from the throng.

And when the new grain comes its hoppers to fill,
How dearly we love the old corn-scented mill.
Hallo, then,—rouse all! Ere the night watch is past,
One more merry round let us have, and the last.
To the ends of each arm!—and now pour in the corn:
The daylight is coming, and we must be gone.
Round with them!—ha, ha! how like willows they spring;
And the sails go down skimming like birds on the wing.
Rise all with them cheerly,—then down let them come:
And now hear the stones, how they sparkle and hum.
As they rapidly swing,
In its fire-circled ring
Each seems like a glad living creature to sing!
Hark, hark, to their song, how it gushes and swells
With sounds like the low, distant chiming of bells.
Once more, all together:—now, up from below;
There is light in the East;—we must go—we must go.

There's a cloud passing by,
Over head in the sky,

And there, for an hour, we our fortune will try ;
It is time to be gone,
For the day will soon dawn,
And the cloud reddens now with the tints of the morn.
It is waiting us there,
And our troop it must bear
On a cool, pleasant sail through the pure morning air.
See, the coming of day,
We must not delay :
Up ! through the blue ether ! up, up, and away !
And now, the old mill
May go on, if it will,—
Or fold up its wings, for a while, and be still.

1839.

SONNET.

ILLUSTRATING A PICTURE.

BY JAMES HOPPIN.

Now bright beneath them gleamed the sunlit vale,
And just discerned, the cot from whence they passed,
When stayed the creaking wheels, and slow and pale
Stepp'd forth the sorrowing emigrants, to cast
Upon the home they left, one gaze,—the last.
The grandsire shaded with his trembling hand
The dim eye, strained upon the roof he reared ;
The son but looked, and bowed himself, unmanned,

Upon his horse's neck, whose rough breast shared
His master's agony ;—unlike the rest
The wife gazed tearless, and her infant son
Folded in silence to her tranquil breast,
As though she felt wherever doomed to roam,
With him and with his sire—*there would be home*.

FADED FLOWERS.

BY SARAH H. WHITMAN.

REMEMBRANCERS of happiness ! to me
Ye bring sweet thoughts of the year's purple prime,
Wild, mingling melodies of bird and bee
That pour on summer winds their silvery chime ;
And of rich incense, burdening all the air,
From flowers that by the sunny garden wall
Bloomed at your side,—nursed into beauty there
By dews and silent showers ; but these to all
Ye bring. Oh ! sweeter far than these the spell
Shrined in those fairy urns for me alone,
For me a charm sleeps in each honied cell
Whose power can call back hours of rapture flown,
To the sad heart sweet memories restore,
Tones, looks and words of love that may return no more.

THE FORSAKEN WIFE.

BY GEORGE W. PATTEN.

'T is past the hour of evening prayer!
What lonely watch is mine!
I hear thy step upon the stair—
No—no—it is not thine;
'T was but a sound the tempest made,
Along the moaning balustrade.

What Circean spells—what Syren charms—
What words of secret art:—
Thus keep thee from my longing arms,
Oh partner of my heart?
And am I not thy chosen bride,
Who—what can take thee from my side?

Soft words may fall from lips refined—
From eyes, soft glances shine:
But 'mid the crowd thou may'st not find,
A heart that loves like mine!
The very tear thy coldness brings
Seems welcome—since for *thee* it springs.

Have I not smil'd when thou wert gay?
Wept—did thy look reprove—
Lov'd thee as *woman sometimes* may,
As *man* can *never* love!

All this—yea more—'twas mine to give ;—
And unrequited—yet I live !

Yet thou didst once with accents bland,
   Beside me bend the knee :
And swear, in truth this little hand,
   Was more than worlds to thee !
This jewell'd hand,—what is it now ?
The token of a broken vow !

Oh love ! How oft the bridal ring,
   Binds fast its golden tie :
To make the heart a slighted thing,
   You pass unheeded by—
The charm is broke—the spell is gone—
And conscious woman weeps alone !

SONNET.

BY WILLIAM J. HOPPIN.

(Suggested by the late disgraceful transactions in Florida.)

Say it in whispers, that the sons of those
   Who fought beside our Fabius, Washington,
   Inheriting a glory, which was won
By honorable port to friends and foes,
Should fling away their birth-right, and enclose
   In a vile ambush that undaunted one,
   Who yielded to their treachery alone.

The arm their valour did not dare oppose !
Hush ! for the Dead at Lexington who sleep,
  The Forlorn-Hope of Freedom must not hear
That our degenerate hands, to which they gave
Truth's spotless banner, all unstained to keep,
  And in her mighty vanguard to uprear,
Have left it buried in a half-breed's grave !
  1838.

TO THE TRAILING ARBUTUS FOUND BLOOMING THROUGH THE SNOW.

BY SAMUEL W. PECKHAM.

I FOUND thee smiling 'mid surrounding gloom,
  While yet the whistling winds their revels kept,
  And nature in the embrace of winter slept ;
Ere spring's sweet songsters had began to plume
Their airy wings : 't was then thy modest bloom
  From underneath the mouldering foliage crept,
  And, as around thy frosty bed I stepped,
The spotless snow seemed almost to assume
  A crimson tint, reflected from thy blush ;
And as I gazed, thy modest beauty gave
  My heart a lesson, and the prayer did gush
That thus I might death's chilling influence brave,
  And that, like thee, my parting soul might flush
With cheerful light the darkness of the grave.

ON SEEING A GRAVE WITHOUT A STONE.

BY PAUL ALLEN.

ALAS ! no scutcheon'd marble here displays,
In long-drawn eulogies, thy name and worth ;
Such servile homage adulation pays
To a poor mouldering clod of common earth.

The pompous eulogy, emblazon'd high,
With all the glare that flattery can bestow,
In splendid falsehood strikes the trav'ler's eye,
And makes the silly tear of pity flow.

The yellow cowslip, and the violet blue,
The pallid daisy, growing by thy side,
Are all, poor peasant ! that remains to you ;
But nature gives what haughty man denied.

Sweet, simple trophies ! and to me more dear
Than all the arrogance of letter'd lore :
Receive the tribute of a parting tear,
Warm from my heart ; a bard can give no more.

STANZAS.

BY JOSIAS L. ARNOLD.

VAIN is the cheek's vermilion hue,
The forehead smooth and high,
The lip, like rose-buds moist with dew,
And vain the sparkling eye.

Vain *beauty's self* the heart to bend,
And in love's fetters bind,
Unless with *grace external* blend
The *graces of the mind.*

The flow'r that's ting'd with various dyes,
At first may lure the eye;
But if no fragrance from it rise,
'T is pass'd neglected by.

1791.

A NOVEMBER LANDSCAPE.

BY SARAH H. WHITMAN.

How like a rich and gorgeous picture hung
In memory's storied hall, seems that fair scene
O'er which long years their mellowing tints have flung;
The way side flowers had faded one by one,
Hoar were the hills, the meadows drear and dun,
When homeward wending 'neath the dusky screen
Of the autumnal woods at close of day,
As o'er a pine-clad height my pathway lay,
Lo! at a sudden turn, the vale below
Lay far outspread all flushed with purple light,
Grey rocks and umbered woods gave back the glow
Of the last day-beams fading into night,
While down a glen where dark Moshassuck flows
With all its kindling lamps the distant city rose.

SPRING.

FROM THE GERMAN OF TIECK, BY HENRY C. WHITAKER.

See, see how the Spring like a glittering bride,
Comes forth on the hills in beauty and pride;
She flings o'er the forest her mantle of green,
Where the blossoming trees so gracefully lean,
And the bird in the branches in merry mood sings,
As he shakes the bright drops of the dew from his wings.
See, see on the soft blushing cheek of the flower,
The red glow grows deeper and deeper each hour;
The winter-frost flies to his cavern so old,
Far down their dark chambers all dismal and cold—
While old earth throws aside his gray robes to the rain
That is falling so gently on river and plain;
And stretches, in joy, his broad arms to embrace
The light form of Spring with her fair smiling face.
Down, down the rough mountains, the silver streams leap
And dance in the valleys so lonely and deep;
No longer the nightingale fears the rude blast,
But sings in the green-wood that winter is past.
Many a shadow grows bright in the beams,
That sparkle and flash from ths swift-bounding streams;
Many a leaf like a diamond gem,
Is waving in beauty on many a stem;
Rainbows are playing on many a flower,
As it lifts its thin petals that drip with the shower;
And the earth, like a monarch, majestic and old,
Sits high on a throne of purple and gold.

THE DEATH BED OF BEAUTY.

BY JAMES O. ROCKWELL.

SHE sleeps in beauty, like the dying rose
  By the warm skies and winds of June forsaken;
Or like the sun, when dimmed with clouds it goes
  To its clear ocean-bed, by calm winds shaken:
Or like the moon, when through its robes of snow
  It smiles with angel meekness—or like sorrow
When it is soothed by resignation's glow,
  Or like herself,—she will be dead to-morrow.

How still she sleeps! The young and sinless girl!
  And the sweet breath upon her red lips trembles!
Waving, almost in death, the raven curl
  That floats around her; and she most resembles
The fall of night upon the ocean foam,
  Wherefrom the sun-light hath not yet departed;
And where the winds are faint! She stealeth home,
  Unsullied girl! an angel broken-hearted!

Oh bitter world! that hadst so cold an eye
  To look upon so fair a type of Heaven;
She could not dwell beneath a winter sky,
  And her heart-strings were frozen here, and riven,
And now she lies in ruins—look and weep!
  How lightly leans her cheek upon the pillow!
And how the bloom of her fair face doth keep
  Changed, like a stricken dolphin on the billow.

LINES.

BY MRS. SOPHIA M. PHILLIPS.

OH know you not, my friends, my friends,
Your faces will arise
On silent wings at evening,
Before my gushing eyes ?
On silent wings at evening,
When I shall long to stand
Beneath the pleasant light of smiles,
Within my own dear land.

I have not loved it well before,
This dearest, greenest spot!
Where nothing now hath ever been
That I remember not.
Oh ! earnest sounds will follow me
Upon the happy breeze ;
Blending of names and voices,
Home music o'er the seas !

And I shall turn me fervently,
To meet its melting power,
And fill with love my yearning soul,
In record of the hour.
And still from each surrounding spell,
My spirit breaking free,
Shall hear and hail forever
This music o'er the sea.

APPENDIX.

Note 1.—Page 29.

In 1724, Dean Berkeley published his proposals for the conversion of the American savages to Christianity, by the establishment of a college in the Bermuda Islands. The plan was very favorably received; and he obtained a charter for a college, in which he was named the first President. He received, also, from Sir Robert Walpole, a promise of a grant of twenty thousand pounds to carry it into effect. He landed at Newport, after a tedious passage of five months, in January, 1729. Soon after his arrival, the Dean purchased a country seat and farm about three miles from Newport, and there erected a house which he named Whitehall. He was admitted a freeman of the Colony, at the General Assembly, in May, 1729. He resided at Newport, about two years and a half, and often preached at Trinity Church. Though he was obliged to return to Europe without effecting his original design, yet his visit was of great utility in imparting an impulse to the literature of our country, particularly in Rhode-Island, and Connecticut. During his residence on the Island of Rhode-Island, he meditated and composed his *Alciphron*, or Minute Philosopher, and tradition says, principally at a place about half a mile southerly from Whitehall. There, in the most elevated part of the Hanging Rocks, (so called) he found a natural alcove, roofed and open to the South, commanding at once a beautiful view of the ocean and the circumjacent islands. This place is said to have been his favorite retreat. His Minute Philosopher was published in London, in 1732, shortly after his return. This acute and ingenious defence of the Christian religion, is written in a series of dialogues, after the model of Plato.

To Bishop Berkeley, the literary institutions of New-England are much indebted. He visited Cambridge, Massachusetts, in 1731, and during his residence at Newport, augmented the library of Harvard College by valuable donations of the Latin and Greek classics. To Yale college, he presented eight hundred and eighty volumes, and, on his departure from Newport, he gave the White-hall estate, consisting of his mansion and one hundred acres of land, for three scholarships in Latin and Greek. After his return to England, in 1733, he sent a magnificent organ, as a donation to Trinity Church, in Newport, which is still in constant use, and bears an inscription which perpetuates the generosity of the donor. —*Elton's Notes to the Memoir of Callender.*

Note 2.—Page 106.

Ezra Stiles, D. D., L. L. D. was the son of the Rev. Isaac Stiles, of North Haven, Connecticut, and was born Dec. 10th, 1727. He graduated at Yale College in 1746, with the reputation of being one of the most accomplished scholars it had ever produced. In 1749, he was chosen one of its tutors, and in that station he remained six years. He was ordained pastor of the second Congregational Church, in Newport, Rhode-Island, the 22d of October, 1755, and continued the able, devoted, and highly esteemed minister of that Church, till he was elected President of Yale College, in 1777. He presided over that institution, with distinguished ability, till his death, May 12th, 1795, in the 68th year of his age. President Stiles was one of the most learned men that our country has ever produced. As a scholar, he was familiar with every department of learning. He had a profound and critical knowledge of the Latin, Greek, French and Hebrew languages; in the Samaritan, Chaldee, Syriac and Arabic he had made considerable progress; and he had bestowed some attention on the Persic and Coptic. He had a passion for history, and an intimate acquaintance with the rabbinical writings and with those of the fathers of the Christian Church. Dr. Stiles maintained an extensive literary correspondence with many eminent persons in remote quarters of the globe; and his name was enrolled as a member of several learned societies in his own and foreign countries. As a preacher, he was impressive and eloquent; and the excellence of his sermons was enhanced by the energy of his delivery, and by the unction which pervaded them. His catholic spirit embraced good men of every nation, sect, and party. In the cause of civil and religious liberty he was enthusiastic.—*Elton's Notes to the Memoir of Callender.*

Note 3.—Page 200.

The author of the Ode to the Poppy, is one of those whom Misery has long since marked for her own, and exercised with the severest forms of physical suffering. Afflicted with a chronic disease, in the seat of thought itself, for which there is no remedy, and which must fatally terminate, through slow and protracted degrees of pain and distress: *never* losing her *consciousness* of present evil, in the balm of *sleep*, the author has yet been able briefly to forget her condition, and to find momentary consolation, in dictating to her friends, several poetical effusions; from which the present has been selected as one of the most finished. Though secluded from the face of Nature, the memory of its various and beautiful forms is quickened, in her solitude, by a poet's imagination. There is a pathos in some of her pieces, a strength of soul struggling against the doom of its decaying tenement, in the agony of deferred and expiring hope, that excite in us, as we lay them down, a feeling of melancholy regret, that another mind is destined to pass away, and leave so imperfect a record of its origin:—a regret that is but partially alleviated by the conviction, however sincere, that, as well in the universe of mind, as of matter, through all their endless changes, nothing is lost; and that all is safe in the hands of its Maker.

The subject of this brief notice is unimproved by *education*, and owes nothing to *circumstances*: thus adding another to the thousand proofs, that *Genius* in its different degrees and kinds, is a *gift*, native in the soul, irrepressible in its growth by the greatest weight of calamity; and flourishing even in the cold shadow of Death.

The author's story disarms criticism, and makes its way at once to the charity of the heart.—*Literary Journal.*

Note 4.—Page 296.

The Poem from which these Stanzas are extracted, was written in Savannah, in 1837, as a description of an entertainment at the hospitable mansion of a gentleman of that city. This fact is mentioned, as nearly the whole Poem, with additions, was published last winter, in a New-York periodical, as a description of a similar entertainment in that city.

Note 5.—Page 321.

In 1836, a book was published in Philadelphia, entitled "Biographical Notes of Commodore Jesse D. Elliot," claiming for that officer the honor of gaining the victory on Lake Erie.

www.ingramcontent.com/pod-product-compliance
Lightning Source LLC
LaVergne TN
LVHW010151110826
845151LV00002B/488